SIMPLY NEGLECT

REDEMPTION BEYOND POVERTY AND FOSTER CARE

LAINIE HARTLEY

WESTBOW
PRESS®
A DIVISION OF THOMAS NELSON
& ZONDERVAN

WestBow Press books may be ordered through booksellers or by contacting:

WestBow Press
A Division of Thomas Nelson & Zondervan
1663 Liberty Drive
Bloomington, IN 47403
www.westbowpress.com
844-714-3454

Front cover photo: White Willow Photography

ISBN: 979-8-3850-2516-9 (sc)
ISBN: 979-8-3850-2517-6 (e)

Library of Congress Control Number: 2024909583

Print information available on the last page.

WestBow Press rev. date: 7/17/2024

Dear Reader,

Before you begin this memoir, please know the journey you are about to embark on contains many difficult and potentially triggering topics. These include physical, emotional, sexual, psychological, and spiritual abuse, as well as domestic violence, neglect, poverty, addiction, and mentions of drugs and alcohol.

I deeply understand how challenging it can be to confront these painful subjects. Therefore, please take care of yourself as you read. If at any moment you find the content overwhelming, please give yourself permission to put the book down and take a break.

I have envisioned your presence beside me throughout the entire writing process, holding your hand through every chapter, staring our pasts in the face, even when it feels like it's burning our eyes. I'm beside you still, working through emotions left in storage, remembering situations rarely talked about to anyone, healing from the inside out, because our journey toward peace and forgiveness is lifelong.

This story, though filled with hardship, is also one of faith, resilience, hope, and triumph. It is my hope that you find solace and inspiration within these words.

We are God's children; we are love, and we are loved. We are seen and forgiven. We belong and we are worthy of our purpose. We are wanted and pursued, restored and redeemed. We can choose joy in a world that seems upside down and still have peace in the storms of our lives. We are fueled with contagious hope. Our experiences hold value, and our achievements are worth celebrating.

Our stories are important.

May our voices be heard.

Love,

Lainie Hartley

CONTENTS

INTRODUCTION

JULY 2015

The thick manila envelope addressed to me by the Toronto Catholic Children's Aid Society feels like hot coal on my bare hands. *Do I rip it open?* My laser stare could burn a hole right through it. I don't know how to proceed. This stack of papers is the first of five files I've received from various children's aid agencies within Ontario. The temptation of unraveling the first nine years of my messy, traumatic life feels equally horrifying and exciting. I want to know who I am, but I also know unveiling these documents comes with hefty consequences. It feels ironic that the papers trapped inside the envelope are so neatly organized but contain only disorder and chaos. I wanted this envelope desperately, but now that it's here, I'm second-guessing my decision.

Being the sixth child of nine, I was unaware Mom was a depressed, anxious, and unmedicated paranoid schizophrenic. I didn't realize my childhood was different from other typical kids'. I was covered in my own waste, living in a cockroach-infested home, starving most of the time, rarely attending school, being shuffled from the projects, to being unhoused in women's shelters and motel rooms.

Did other children long to be shown the love of a mother and father the same way I did?

I sway my one-year-old daughter, Olivia, back and forth on my hip. Violet, who I birthed twelve short months earlier, is crying at my feet and pulling on my pant leg, letting me know she wants to be held too.

"It's okay, sweetheart. Mommy's here."

I toss the envelope upside-down on the kitchen table and lift Violet to join her sister in my arms. Being a loving wife to my husband, Levi, and a safe, present, and nurturing mother to our girls is all I hoped for. As I continue to sway both girls from side to side, their heavy eyes and drooping heads fall to my chest. The paradox of grief and gratitude consistently show up in my life; I'm tending to my babies needs while glaring at a file full of heartbreaking records with written proof of all the ways Mom couldn't care for me. I make a quiet shushing noise between the girls' ears, then lay them in their cribs for their afternoon nap.

I start the kettle to make some tea. I grab my favorite mug and all the fixings, then wait for the kettle's whistle. I look around the house and notice all the projects needing to be finished. Levi works away from home during the week and he's coming home tonight. I can't wait to see him.

I receive my dream job working for the school board as an educational assistant, supporting special needs children and youth with their learning. I love my job and the people I work with. After long workdays, my evenings are full of dinner preparations, cleanups, housework, baths, bedtime routines, and getting the girls to sleep. I hate sleeping without Levi during the week because of nightmares and night terrors I have. I haven't been sleeping well, and not having the man I love and trust the most beside me makes them worse.

I'm wondering whether I'm in a proper mental state to delve into these files. I bite my inner cheek and clench my jaw—something I do so often I don't realize I'm doing it anymore. I consciously take a deep breath in and exhale. I should wait until Levi gets home.

This file, whether good or bad, is the bridge to my past. It's also my first and only childhood possession. Mom didn't take photos of me as a child, and because we moved so much, nothing stayed with me. The clerk from CCAS Disclosure Services tells me over the phone there are photos of me enclosed in my file, but they're sadly almost completely obscured and of poor quality as a result of being photocopied so many years ago. I am disappointed but eager to see them anyway.

This has to be done. I need to understand who I was to understand who I am, to know why I'm struggling so hard mentally, so I can defeat the darkness and become the best version of myself, and so I can stop resisting the little girl living within me.

After making my tea, I toss my hair up into a ponytail. I grab the wrinkled envelope from the table and bring it to my bedroom. I decide to embrace every word in the file and give myself permission to feel every raw emotion I need to feel.

"God, who am I? Why did you give me this life? Show me who I am in these pages. Show me who you are and where you were through it all."

I unveil the contents, and already the first paragraph makes me nervous: "It has been our experience that reviewing this type of information can surface many emotions for people and I would urge you to seek support from people you can trust."

I scoff. As a child, I was supposed to feel safe under the care of their agency. I find it infuriating that, after so many years, they finally seem to care how I feel. I skim the first few pages. The workers who documented my childhood spoke words that hurt me: "Filthy, disgusting, bizarre, animal-like behavior, out of control, wild, unruly, covered in feces, smelled of urine, unkempt, dirty looking ..."

I was more than that, I think to myself.

I want to add words to the page: "Lainie is a resilient and happy little girl. She is a great sister. Lainie loves with all her heart."

I was so much more than the way I looked. I was so much more than my behavior. Didn't the professionals reporting against me know I was saying something with the way I acted? I was fighting for survival.

I turned back to the page, but the words from my file have become a jumbled, painful mess to read. It pains me even further to know that the stories I'm reading actually happened. I have questioned my childhood experiences up until this point. *I'm probably overexaggerating. There's no way my mom would do that.* My hands clench together and turn pale. I remember what I'm reading. I see it all again, and I relive harrowing scenarios. My breathing shallows. The black letters escape the pages in front of me and rapidly spin like a tornado above my head that is pulling everything into its eye and destroying anything in its path.

I feel the pain of my inner child as she pounds the walls of my heart with her fists. I am overcome with emotion. I imagine our two daughters wandering alone in our crime-ridden neighborhood, filthy, hungry, and begging for food and affection. The vision breaks me. I would go to the depths of the earth to protect our girls and make sure they're provided for. I press my hand firmly against my chest and concentrate on my breathing to reel my anxious thoughts back to the present moment.

I feel angry at my mother for leaving me unsafe and vulnerable, for being selfish and making poor decisions, for repeatedly putting me in harm's way, and for giving me to people who damaged me further. I wish I had been born to a mother who showed she loved me and a father who stayed long enough to know me. I'm angry at a foster care system that was supposed to protect me but chose to prolong my hardships and ultimately gave up on our family because of how much work we were. I'm sorry to my younger self, who experienced so much trauma and never spoke to a counselor or anyone who could help me understand my thoughts or feelings.

Society tells me it's shameful to talk about these things, so I keep it to myself. Growing up, I was expected to stay silent about foster care and failed kinship placements because I was supposed to be grateful to those who opened their home to me, even if they treated me terribly. I was reprimanded for speaking about how damaging and abusive the church can be. I was to be submissive and protective of church leaders and their reputations, even at the expense of my own. I certainly wasn't supposed to talk negatively about my mother, because it would hurt her heart and my siblings' feelings. Society shames vulnerability. Speaking truthfully about the wreckage of inner trauma is considered baggage. I'm presumed to walk upright, bearing the weight of shame others have dumped on my back, along with my own. It isn't right. This is why so many hurting people stay quiet. How is one possibly supposed to hold on to all this pain alone?

Forget what society says. I can't be silent anymore.

Living in the heaviness of trauma feels like treading water in an ocean with weights around my ankles. My head is barely above the surface, and I'm tired and worn. I know I can't survive this way much longer. I'm in desperate need of rescue. My anxious mind awaits answers to the questions that plague my heart.

- Is it possible to heal from my childhood trauma?
- Can I be a good wife and mother when I've never seen doing so modeled in a healthy way?
- Can I stop generational pain from continuing forward in my children's lives?
- Is there purpose in my pain?
- Can I forgive my mother for the times she gave me away?
- Can I forgive my biological father for abandoning me?
- Can I forgive the abusers of my childhood?
- How do I deconstruct religious trauma?
- How do I get the attention of a massively broken government agency that reports heavily on the neglect it sees but chooses not to act when its job is to protect children like me? How can I bring attention to their failings and change the way it functions?

I need answers to the questions barricading my mind. For me, that means starting from the beginning.

CHAPTER ONE

Regent Park (1986–1991)

… August 11, 1988. No windows were open despite the excessive heat. The apartment was "filthy and infected with flies and roaches." Heavy blankets covered the windows. No lights were on, and the apartment was lit only by the light from the television. The five children were described as filthy.

—CCAS report, 1988

Toronto Police called as they had visited the home at 12:06am that morning as a result of a domestic complaint. The officer was very disturbed by the very bad unsanitary conditions in the home – smelly, lots of flies and concerned for the well-being of the children.

—CCAS report, 1988

The children were wild; they don't like to wear clothes.

—CCAS report, 1988

My grubby young toes narrowly miss the swing of the half-hinged bedroom door as Mom's foul-mouthed, heavy-breathing abuser shoves my body onto the urine-filled laundry pile inside. His evil eyes are small and lifeless, and his pupils are dilated. He threatens he'll beat me and my siblings if we leave this room. He slams the door behind him and immediately goes to find our mother in the living room, where the screaming and grunting begins instantly.

The bedroom feels big when I stand in it alone but sitting here with my four siblings on this mountain of soiled laundry makes it feel small and claustrophobic. I'm barely three years old and not potty trained yet. I've peed on this laundry pile several times before. My siblings do the same because we can't use our bathroom toilet. It's been clogged for weeks and overflows when flushed. Mom is unfazed by the maggots and rotting clothes that cover the bathroom floor and still bathes in the tub daily.

My sister Rachel is cooking her younger siblings instant macaroni on a hot plate plugged into the wall. "Try not to listen to them, sweetie," she says as she rubs my cheek. I lean into her. She's ten years older than I am and is like a mother to me and my younger sister, Ellie, who's only a year and a half. Mom has seven children, and an eighth baby on the way. The two oldest, Colleen and Lonnie Jr., have left home already, but Rachel won't leave her younger siblings, as she feels responsible to care for Mom and her children. She's only thirteen, the same age Colleen was when Mom kicked her out two years ago.

I lie in Rachel's lap and look up to the clouds of spiders crowding in the corners of the ceiling and watch the cockroaches climb the walls. I imagine they're in a race against each other, and I cheer for the contestants. I can feel the lumps of dead mice buried beneath the clothes that make my skin feel itchy. The other units in our building have cockroaches, spiders, and flies too, but because of Mom's lack of cleanliness, and her wild and untamed children, our unit is home to thousands of skittering creepy crawlers. Rachel says there are over a hundred mice that hide in the walls during the day and venture into our unit at night. They run across our filthy floors, and by our feet when we sit on the couch, and dead ones lie in the gaps between the cushions. The critters, though not invited, have made our apartment their home, much like the men who abuse my mother.

My brothers devour their macaroni and are instantly bored. They jump out through the brittle forty-year-old window to find friends or something to do in the neighborhood. Rachel reaches for Ellie and pulls her cheesy face close to her chest as we snuggle and wait for the front door of our apartment to slam closed. That's how we know he's gone.

"We want to come out!" Rachel yells. "We've been in here forever!"

Mom opens the door. "I can't even make love to my boyfriend without you complaining!" Mom screams into the bedroom. "You're just jealous! You want him for yourself, don't you?"

I look up into Rachel's eyes and lean into her again. She's unfazed by Mom's words. I hate when Mom talks to her like that.

I'm a scrawny and scrappy three-year-old little girl with the mouth of an angry sailor and full of fight in my little bones. My hair is a deep chestnut brown, and my full, round face is always filthy. All my tiny teeth are rotten as a result of nursing bottle cavities. Mom can't afford to buy milk, so she mixes cups of white sugar with warm water in baby bottles and gives that to me instead. We live in Regent Park, Toronto, Ontario, the first and largest social housing project in Canada and the second largest in all North America. We're in a run-down apartment complex with my undiagnosed paranoid schizophrenic mother, Annie Andrews; my older sister, Rachel; my two older brothers, Blaire and Dylan; my younger sister, Ellie; and various abusive men who visit Mom at their convenience. Garbage, debris, and infested mattresses are pushed over tenants' railings. The dumpsters are overflowing and spilling into the back alleys and streets. The filth here is toxic and overwhelming.

The violence in Regent Park is inescapable. The sixty-nine acres of isolated land without any through traffic oozes like an infected wound of poverty and crime. Emergency vehicles are limited in accessing the park, which creates horrifying opportunities for gangs, violence, sexual assaults, drug deals, and murders. Danger is outside each door, in the hallways, the stairwells, the sidewalks, the parks, and the homes of residents—residents who know to lock their doors and never answer to anyone knocking. Regent is ranked one of the most dangerous places to live in Canada, and it's the place I call home.

Our six-story red-brick apartment complex, known as "Block 1," stands on the busy street corners of Parliament and Oak. Our building, along with every other housing unit in Regent Park, needs immediate, extensive repair. The stench upon entering is mostly of cheap alcohol, old tobacco, and the stale urine of drunks who stumble along the hallways. The strips of wallpaper dangle with exhaustion from their effort to escape the yellow, nicotine-stained drywall, and the only artwork displayed is the fist-sized holes that make a perfect entrance for the mice and roaches that try to evict us. They're also a reminder of the angry men who crawl through our windows and barge through our doors to make our living room their personal wrestling ring.

Our apartment is on the ground floor and makes us vulnerable to intruders. I never know when angry men full of drugs or alcohol will enter. My body is on high alert, and my legs are prepared to run and hide with Rachel at any moment. My older brothers come and go through our living room windows like puppies through a doggy door. It's funny to watch them do it, but not so funny when men do it. The windows give birth to them often, and they land on our floor with a thud. Our front door has been lunged at and broken several times. Rachel puts furniture behind it, hoping a barricade will keep them out. She then places wood on each window track around the apartment. At night, she chains all four of our bedroom doors together and brings us to the living room to sleep with her.

Men are infatuated with Mom. She tells us they love her, and she does whatever they ask her to do. They get angry and abuse her in front of us when she tells them no. They dehumanize her and treat her like a dog. It's common for Mom and men to be intimate together in front of us. They are never discreet. Rachel throws cooked oatmeal wrapped in wet toilet paper at their moving bodies, but Mom ignores her daughter's oatmeal bombs and doesn't stop.

Rachel's compliance began when she was only five years old. She realized she could earn Mom's love by being her little helper. One night, Mom realized she didn't have any milk for Blaire's bedtime bottle. She had asked her two oldest, Colleen and Lonnie Jr., who were seven and six years old, to return a bunch of canned tomatoes to the grocery store, which was a forty-five-minute walk away. Mom wanted them to exchange the tomatoes for milk, but because it was dark out, they both said no.

"I'll go, Mom." Rachel said eagerly. Mom beamed with pride toward Rachel and talked affectionately to her. Rachel felt ten feet tall to have Mom speak so positively to her. She felt responsible to care for her one-year-old brother. Mom loaded the canned tomatoes in a metal cart and sent her five-year-old daughter on a two-hour journey through Regent Park. Miraculously, Rachel made it home with the milk, unharmed. From then on, Rachel did everything for Mom.

Rachel tried to make Mom proud even after several years of being belittled by her. As Rachel grew older, Mom realized her daughter's youthful beauty was a detrimental distraction to the men in her life. She became jealous and blamed Rachel when something went wrong between her and a man. She spoke to every flaw she believed Rachel had to break her self-esteem. As usual, Rachel reassured Mom that Mom was the beautiful one and promised she wanted nothing to do with the men in her life.

Mom doesn't have two coins to rub together, because she was never taught how to budget. She's terrible with money. There is a No Frills grocery store nearby that always has great deals, but Mom says its name means "nothing fancy," and she refuses to be labeled as such. Mom wants groceries from the high-end Dominion, which is far away, and even pays for a taxi both ways. Following in her older siblings' footsteps, Rachel now hustles deals all over town to provide for our family when we have no money: the grocery stores, the restaurants, and the streets. She knocks on doors and asks people for money. At Christmastime, she sings carols to the residents of the apartment complex. After school, she collects glass pop bottles and beer cans. The cans aren't worth as much as the bottles, but there are more of them.

Rachel tells Mom she'd like to help her by getting the family's groceries and cashing her welfare checks. Mom is thrilled and easily persuaded that Rachel enjoys helping her, but the truth is, Rachel is tired of the family being starving and broke and knows she can plan Mom's money better than she could.

Rachel takes me most places she goes. She buckles me in grocery carts and plays peek-a-boo with me as she leans around my small body to see ahead of her. She's still a child herself. Other times, she straps me in my umbrella stroller while she runs errands around town. I giggle when she crosses over the metal streetcar tracks, because the rhythmic bumps make my voice sound funny.

Rachel's responsibilities are burdensome and should be fulfilled by Mom. She lives every day in survival mode. She takes care of all of us, including our mother, and I'm attached to her like glue. She feeds me, clothes me, changes my diapers, and gets me ready for appointments. She plays with me, cares for me, and never leaves my side. Rachel is my place of safety, my guardian, and my protector.

CHAPTER TWO

Don't Follow Me Out of Here (1988–1991)

On August 19, 1988 the Society worker visited the home. It was apparent an attempt had been made to clean up, however, the children were "filthy." It became apparent that an older sibling was parenting the children and their caregiver. In September <u>the apartment did not meet the minimal standards for living</u>. Neighborhood complaints increased regarding the children's out-of-control behavior in the building. Several meetings were held with the school and community services to attempt to make a consistent effort to assist the family. Over the next several months, the situation deteriorated, particularly the supervision of the children. Two of (Lainie's) siblings received injuries due to lack of supervision.

—CCAS report, 1988

(Lainie) cried and resisted separation from her mother and sister.

—CCAS report, 1990

The CCAS didn't remove Blaire after he received dozens of stitches from his wrist up toward his elbow, nearly bleeding out from a failed attempt at escaping his frozen forty-year-old bedroom window. They didn't remove him after suffering second degree burns that bubbled and blistered before our eyes after inadvertently stepping backward into a baby basin he filled with scalding water (that had yet to be fixed by a repairman) to wash the floors of his bedroom, aiming to replicate the squeaking sound of sneakers he heard walking around at the hospital. They didn't remove him either time after spending weeks recovering alone in the hospital. But when Mom called the CCAS to take her kids, they did.

The workers arrive at our apartment shortly after Mom's call and surprise Blaire with the news that he's leaving immediately. Blaire realizes what is happening and begs Mom to stay with his family. Blaire is standing at the door screaming, saying he won't be bad anymore.

"That's what he always says," Mom states, agitated. "Take him." She's frustrated with his accidents and doesn't want to handle the chaos he causes.

Just like that, my big brother is gone, and I don't know where he's going or when I'll see him again.

Before leaving our apartment, the worker exclaims, "The physical condition of your home is unacceptable, your kids have absolutely no structure or routine, and their behavior is incredibly bizarre. They're a bunch of unruly wild animals and need psychological testing done immediately."

Mom closes the door and sits on the couch. I can still hear my brother screaming for her down the hall. I wonder whether she'll call and ask them to take me next. I conclude I had better be a good girl.

Life at home doesn't change without my brother home. On June 24, 1989, my baby sister Rosie is born. Mom asks the CCAS to put my brother Dylan, me, and Ellie into a foster home for ten days while she recovers from birth. It feels good to be out of our filthy home, but the foster home feels and looks so different. The house is clean. The mother tells us we're in foster care and will go home in ten days, and we do.

After returning home from foster care, I go with Mom and my siblings to a doctor's appointment at the Family Practice Unit. Our doctor says he and another doctor are well acquainted with the numerous problems with our family and talks about how difficult and chaotic it is to examine us. It's true. I throw my body down to the floor when he tries to touch me and resist at all costs while screaming for help. When I realize he isn't trying to hurt me, I soften and show him I'm a sweet, loving girl beneath my temper tantrums and rage.

He tells Mom I'm delayed in my speech, my temper tantrums are a problem, I need to start toilet training, and he can't examine my ears because they're thickly plugged with wax. I have a lot of problems with my ears. They hurt all the time, and I can barely hear. The doctor tells Mom a hearing test is most important and makes an appointment for me to see an audiologist in September. Mom brings me in November. The doctor tells her I have a lot of fluid in my ears and I need another follow-up appointment in six months. She doesn't take me.

Rosie is three months old and incredibly sick with vomiting and diarrhea. She's failing to thrive, and Mom is really worried about her baby. Mom takes Rosie to the hospital to have her examined, and workers are immediately concerned about her declining health. They notify CCAS, who come to the hospital right away and take her from Mom's arms. Mom comes home without her baby, and just like that, my sister is gone too. Mom tells me she went to a foster home and isn't sure when she'll be back.

That same month, Ellie and I are picked up by our mom's brother and his wife, Steve, and Lisa Thompson, to spend ten days with them and their two sons at their house in Barrie. Lisa makes me feel special. She bathes me and picks the bugs from my scalp while she brushes my hair. She feeds me and tucks me in at night and prays softly to a "Dear Jesus." I like spending time with her. She doesn't have any daughters but I think she'd like to someday.

Mom takes me, Dylan, and Ellie to Nellie's Hostel in October for several days. Rachel has left home for a while, and Blaire is still gone. The housing authority is at our apartment, taking pictures to begin the process of eviction. Mom tells me it means we aren't allowed to go back home. We live among the poorest people in Toronto and are getting evicted from the slums. Our family is now unhoused, but we're happy to leave Regent Park. I hope Mom's abusers forget about her and don't know where we are. I think maybe they'll disappear and be gone for good.

It's January 1990, the beginning of a fresh new year and the middle of a freezing cold Canadian winter. I'm out for a walk with Mom, Rachel, and Ellie—which is odd because Mom doesn't usually come with us. I study Mom's posture as she walks ahead of us with determination in her steps. I sense that whatever we're doing or wherever we're going must be important. Her straw-like hair sits just past her shoulders. She hates her ears and makes sure they're always covered. Her shoulders are slouched, and her full face of makeup stares toward the ground.

The sun is shining and makes the icicles on the trees look like dancing crystals. I pull one off a low-hanging branch and suck on it. The cold snow crunches beneath our ripped shoes. It's a perfect day for a snowball fight. Rachel rubs her thumbs on both my and Ellie's hands as she grips them and pulls us close. I glance at her face and notice she's crying. Something doesn't feel right.

Mom walks us up a path leading to a large building and tells the people inside with name tags that they're putting too much pressure and responsibility on her as a mother. She tells them she's leaving "the girls" here. I think about what she's said. Mom refers to me and Ellie as the girls, and I wonder whether she's talking about us. Rachel's eyes fill with tears, and she begins to weep uncontrollably. Mom's whole body is twitching as if she's being shocked. She's frustrated. My thirteen-year-old sister is suddenly expected to hand over the little sisters she's raised.

"I'm so sorry, girls," Rachel sobs. "I begged Mom to change her mind and keep you, but she can't. I wish I could, but I can't either. We need to be apart for a while."

"You going?" I ask.

"Yes, you're staying here, Lainie, and we're leaving," Mom says flatly.

Panic. My heart races and heat fills my body. My brain tries to make sense of what's happening.

"You going?" I ask again. "And come back?"

Rachel wipes her face with the sleeve of her coat. "No, Lainie. I don't know when I'll see you again."

"I go with you?" I grab hold of Rachel's leg with both arms and feet. "You *not* going, Rachel. You stay here. With me."

The workers peel me off Rachel's leg. "You both should leave now," one of them says, "before this gets out of hand."

I'm physically picked up against my will and taken from my sister's leg. It sends me into hysteria, a full-body panic. Mom's eyes hold no emotion as she turns to walk away from me. "Don't follow us out of here."

"I love you girls so much," Rachel says, weeping, as she turns to follow Mom out of the building.

I'm waiting for Rachel to turn around, grab our hands, and walk out with us together. But she doesn't. I do everything I can to run to her, but the worker catches me and calls other workers for help.

"I go with you!" I plead. "Take me with you! Get me. Pick me up. Please, Rachel! No go! No leave me here!" I collapse to the floor, kicking and screaming, resisting the separation. I'm in shock. Ellie watches my tantrum, completely unaware of what's happening. My body gives up the fight. I feel dead inside. I feel nothing.

Ellie and I are stripped of our nasty clothes, buckled into a van nearly naked, and brought by a stranger to a home that isn't ours, to live with kids who aren't our siblings. I'm scared. I don't know where I am or what is happening.

I arrive at our new foster home and wail nonstop for Mom and Rachel with loud, ear-piercing, torturous cries. My foster mother sends me to my room and says no one in the house wants to hear those awful sounds. It's the only way I know how to get what I want, but it's not working right now. Mom caves to it all the time. I can't hold on to this pain I feel inside. I hate being in bedrooms alone and don't want to be in here. The foster mother tells me I'm welcome to join the family when I stop scaring everyone with my bloodcurdling screeches.

"Please don't lock the door," I say desperately before she turns to walk away.

"Your door is open, sweetheart. You're welcome to join the family when you've calmed down."

I need to be held, but I'm too young to voice my needs. I don't know Bee that well. I need Rachel to hold me. I need to be with my family. Instead I am alone with my tears, my thoughts, and my aching heart. I stop crying and think heavily about how to get me and Ellie back to Mom and Rachel.

I am thrilled when Bee tells me and my sister that we'll have visits with Mom every week. I am always excited to see Mom, but I'm frazzled and distressed when we have to say good-bye. I don't understand why we can't leave together. Bee tells us that after a few months, we'll get to stay with Mom for an entire weekend. Bee is good to me and Ellie, and she treats us well. Like Steve and Lisa, she doesn't have any daughters either. She has three sons right now, and they're so much fun to play with. Bee quickly discovers my love for fashion and buys me colorful dresses and clothes that make me feel like a magazine model. I beg her to take me to get my ears pierced, and she does. I love wearing earrings, especially when she takes us to church on Sundays. She styles my mushroom-cut hair as best she can and buys me headbands I wear like crowns. I feel like a princess. Ellie is never far from my side and enjoys getting dolled up too.

I have a lot of appointments in foster care. My upcoming appointment includes me going to a dental clinic at the Hospital for Sick Children to remove my rotten teeth. The dentist warns me that what he needs to do in my mouth is "extensive" and encourages me to be brave. I tell him I'm fearless. I resolve that I'm going to prove my high pain tolerance so he doesn't think I'm a wimp. He numbs my mouth with a long needle and proceeds to pull several teeth. I don't move a muscle or flinch. He is shocked by my mental and physical stamina; his encouraging words make me feel like the strongest kid around. He raises my chair into a sitting position and pats me on the back. I move my tongue all around my empty mouth and feel every tender empty hole. He grabs the mirror from the counter and holds it in front of my face. I pull my lips apart with my fingers and am horrified to see my toothless, shining gums under the light. I look like an old chimpanzee from the zoo. I look at the dentist with desperation in my eyes. He looks over to Bee, who covers her mouth and tries not to giggle. "It looks so much better, sweetheart." I'm not convinced. The dentist sucks his lips inside his mouth and holds them together with his teeth. He looks away from Bee and faces me. I squint my eyes toward him because I know he wants to laugh too. Before I know it, my shining gums open and make way for the purest laugh I've had in a long time. When we all settle, he helps me out of the chair and wishes me well before I go.

It's May 1990, the month I turn four years old, and Bee is hosting my very first birthday party with cake, ice cream, and wrapped presents. My cake has my name and candles on it, and I can't wait to blow them out. It feels extraordinary to have people celebrating my life with gifts and treats.

Our visits with Mom are drastically increased in June. We now stay with her for the entire week and return to Bee's on the weekends. Whenever Ellie and I return to Bee's house after visiting Mom, she strips us of our clothes at the door, brushes the squished cockroaches from our feet, and puts us into the bath right away. I love the feeling of being clean and cared for.

Dylan was sent into foster care after we were removed from Mom but has since returned home with Blaire. I am elated to know that Blaire, Dylan, and Rosie are home now and instantly feel like the two walls of my heart are being forced to fight against each other. I am willing to do whatever I can to get back home to my family, but I love my life here with Ellie, Bee, and her sons. Rachel had no children to be responsible for when Mom's kids were in foster care. She wanted a better life for herself and decided to leave home for good. My heart is crushed yet again to imagine my life without her taking care of me every day. Without her home, it will be my responsibility to care for Ellie and Rosie. I can't take care of Rosie while living with Bee, so I invite Bee to live with us. I'm heartbroken when she kindly declines.

Bee tells us we're going on vacation this summer. I don't know what that means, but we're leaving the house. She packs up the family vehicle and drives us to her parent's lakefront cottage, where Ellie and I spend hours and hours jumping off the dock with her boys. When we aren't in the water, we're riding our bikes or catching frogs and bugs in the bushes. We finish the nights watching the sunsets over the lake and roasting marshmallows over an open fire. Ellie and I are having the best time. While we'll remember this experience forever, our hearts still ache to be reunified with our family.

In December 1990, when Ellie and I have been living with Bee for a year now, off and on, the CCAS driver picks me and Ellie up from Bee's to go visit Mom. After our visit, the driver tries to get me into the vehicle, but I refuse and throw a big temper tantrum. He threatens to leave me on the ground screaming, but it's exactly what I want him to do. Mom stands by watching me tantrum and doesn't do a thing to prevent me from leaving with him. The driver calls the CCAS office and argues into the phone about me, saying I'm always unbuckling my seatbelt and trying to jump out of his vehicle, even when he's driving. He screams into the phone that he isn't about to drive this devil child anywhere and hangs up on them. He leaves me screaming on the ground, as he said he would, and drives off. I jump up, wipe my eyes, hug my sister, and ask Mom whether we can go get some food. Ellie and I, sadly, never return to Bee's foster home.

Now that I'm back home, I'm not sure throwing a temper tantrum to stay with Mom was the right decision. I'm hoping Rachel will find out I'm home again and return to me. I'm happy to be reunited with my ever-torn family, but I already miss my life with Bee, her family, and the privileges I had while living with them. I know that Bee has Christmas presents under the tree for me and Ellie, and we won't be there to open them with her on Christmas morning. I don't know how to feel. I want to live with all the people I love. The chaos of life with Mom was the only normal I knew until I stayed with Bee. The realization that not everyone lives the way my family does has me confused. There are calm, functioning people who live very different lives than ours—lives that include peace, provision, and safety. I miss having clean clothes and wearing pretty dresses. I miss the trips to the lake, relaxing at their cottage, and having three meals a day. I miss the attention and love from Bee.

In August 1991, Mom, Blaire, Dylan, I, Ellie, and Rosie head to the women's shelter. They help our family move into a run-down double-bed motel room at the Gateway Inn and give our family a daily food allowance of $26.50. Every day, we race to the front desk of the motel and collect the money as if we've just won the lottery. We have exactly enough money for two large pizzas and six cans of Coke, which is what we consume almost daily. Mom and Blaire have the splitting up of food down to a science.

Finally, after three months of living in a run-down motel, a housing unit becomes available in Scarborough. We move in on Halloween night, 1991, which feels ironic because we're sure this house is haunted.

CHAPTER THREE

Scarborough, Toronto, Ontario (October 1991–December 1994)

In June 1993 the Society received a report regarding allegations that the children were constantly dirty and always begging their neighbors for food. The file was closed as it appeared to be an invalid complaint.
—CCAS report, 1993

The caregiver appeared to need food.
—CCAS report, 1993

… they frequently went to neighbors to ask for food and over the past weekend, one of the children went to the neighbors at midnight to get food.
—CCAS report, 1994

The CRW (Community Relations Worker) stated a maintenance employee reported there was human waste all over and the caregiver was given four weeks to clean it up. One month earlier, the children were dumping clothes on the street.
—CCAS report, 1994

The housing complex in Scarborough is known for its diverse culture and is only ten kilometers down the road from Regent Park. Our house is part of two rows of identical connected units that face each other across a rectangular parking lot.

The state of our house makes my stomach turn. We children are so out of control that not even the four walls of our home can cage us. Anyone who is brave enough to enter keeps his or her shoes on. As soon as the door opens to our crumbling, forsaken unit, the smell is strong enough to blow you backward and send you running outside for fresh air. Inside, the heavy, stinking air sits like weights on our lungs, making us feel like asthmatics without inhalers. The floor is covered in urine-stained clothes, human waste, garbage, and food that rotted weeks before.

Mom keeps the windows covered with comforters and heavy blankets. She sits in the darkened living room, watching our big, fuzzy television, the kind you leave the couch for to turn the dial. She gets around with only the glow it provides. When we turn the lights on, mice scatter and dart in every direction and thousands of skittering cockroaches race across the walls and counters, frantically looking for a new dark place to take shelter. They are in every crevice. My siblings and I pull them out of each other's ears, off the bottoms of our feet, and, when we eat, out of our food. There are so many it makes me think we're guests in their home.

Another reason Mom hangs thick heavy blankets over the windows is to keep spirits out of the apartment. I find it strange that she tries to keep them out, because she sits us all in the living room with several candles lit and invites them in. Maybe she thinks the spirits she's inviting in are good ones. She calls out names and asks the spirits to show us they're there. With no airflow through our house, the candle flames sway back and forth as if someone is blowing out a trick candle on a birthday cake. When they completely blow out, it sends us straight for the door and into the streets, screaming.

The spirits are playing tug-of-war with Mom's sanity. Mom's green eyes are usually focused on the television set and not on us. It's an uncomfortable and scary feeling when she stares at us. She sits on the edge of the couch, glaring intensely at my brothers' rubber toy wrestlers Ellie and I are playing with. She leans forward with her hands on her knees, looking like a lioness about to devour her prey. Her eyes darken and are no longer green. I feel hot when her eerie glare fastens on me. She darts toward us, and we scream midbreath, falling to our backs like turtles and kicking our feet for protection from her.

"They're haunted! Don't touch them! They're from the devil!" she shouts.

She picks up the wrestlers and throws them right out the second-story window. Mom says they levitate in the air at night. I jump to my feet, my face still red and hot, and run out of the room. I don't want to play with haunted toys. I don't want Mom looking at me like that any longer either.

My tantrums happen anytime, anywhere. If I am upset, I throw my raging body to the ground in a full-on temper tantrum, kicking my feet, flailing my arms, and making people's ears ring with my torturous screams. I lie on the metal streetcar tracks in the middle of Toronto's insanely busy traffic and refuse to get up until I get my way. My mother cannot handle me, and I infuriate her.

I shout for food nonstop in the middle of the night while Mom sits and watches her television shows in the dark. I scream louder when she ignores me. I know it makes her mad, but it gets her attention; she hates it when I interrupt her shows. Unable to handle my ear-piercing cries, Mom angrily gets up from the couch, marches toward me, and points her finger at me as if she's just drawn a sword. She's face-to-face with me, looking into my eyes, spitting her angry words at me like a spray pump across my small, freckled face.

I just want some food.

Mom finally goes to the dark kitchen and makes me boxed macaroni and cheese. When she brings it out, I stop screaming. When I look down to scoop my second bite, I see boiled cockroaches in my bowl. I throw it and scream. The roaches always seem to serve themselves first, and I hate it. Mom's angry that I've thrown my food and hits me on the side of my head repeatedly, making my ears ring. She rips me from the couch with fists full of my matted hair and drags me across the room like a rag doll. It's past midnight, and I'm too tired to search for food. I rub my head to comfort myself and feel the throbbing sting of the goose egg rising beneath my scalp. I fall asleep from exhaustion and wake the next morning, starving.

I look on the stove and find the pot of macaroni Mom cooked the night before. There inside the pot is a small, bloated mouse lying on its back with its mouth open, displaying its two little buck teeth. I'm not sure if it's dead from natural causes or still in a food coma.

That night, Mom sends me and Ellie upstairs to have a bath together. We race up the old, creaking steps, pull the tub's dial from the wall, and get undressed. We quickly jump into the scalding water, then immediately tumble from the bathtub to the floor, holding our stinging red ankles. We turn the dial all the way to the right and wait for the cold water to even out the temperature. We push our feet beneath the tap and slide backward and forward over and over again, making waves in the tub and soaking the floor. We throw our heads back, laughing. Ellie and I notice a shape, like an ethereal figure of a person, moving around in the top left corner of the bathroom. We blink hard again and again to make sure it isn't the water in our eyes. We hear the stairs creak but know no one is on them. We jump out of the tub and run downstairs naked, screaming that we've seen ghosts in the bathroom and can hear them running on our stairs.

Mom is on her back in the living room with another man we don't know. Ellie and I stand in front of them, naked, wet and cold, narrating our scary ghost story, totally unfazed by what they're doing. Mom listens to us tell the story while the man keeps pushing into her body. Mom and the man who brings us chips are neither concerned nor interested in our story and tell us to go back upstairs.

CHAPTER FOUR

Daydreamer (1991–1995)

The file was closed at which time the Society worker wrote, "This is a family which is functioning on the margins of what is acceptable in terms of childcare and child safety. At this time, the problems are not severe enough to warrant CCAS involvement."
—CCAS report, October 1994

Our cement porch has an enclosed storage space about four feet tall and three feet wide. The empty, abandoned area is meant for storing garbage—ironic, since I feel like garbage too. Mom doesn't clean and has no use for it, so I claim it for myself. I pretend it's my home, my place of safety, my dreaming box. Mom's abusers rest their elbows on it, and I can see their knees through the cracks from the inside.

The deteriorating dark green wooden doors loosely hold black metal handles that rattle. It's a brilliant place to hide on the mornings when I refuse to go to school. I sit in there quietly, hugging my knees to my chest and chewing my hair as I always do. The sun sends its rays through the wooden cracks of the doors and across my face, connecting to the core of my being and warming my body with its embrace. I breathe better in its glow. I want the sun's rays to erase the dark shadows from my face so I can become fully radiant, as I am in my dreams. Oh, my dreams; they are real to me even when I'm wide awake.

I dream of a father loving me like his own. I want to feel safe with someone who is gentle with his hands and doesn't hurt me, my mom, or my family.

Why don't I deserve that? What is it about me that makes me so unlovable? Am I not cute enough? Am I too loud? Or am I just in the way? I feel invisible.

The front door flings open, making me jump. Mom is standing on the porch, screaming to the wind. "Lainie! Get in the house! *Now!*" I don't say a word and hug my knees a little tighter. After a few seconds, Mom goes back inside. I continue to nervously chew my hair, play with the crawling ants, pick at my scabs, and scratch at the peeling paint on the door.

The school counselor approaches our front porch and opens the decaying doors. "Hi, sweetheart," she says, crouching down to my level with a smile. "What are you doing here?"

"I'm dreaming." I say.

"Well, you're late to school again. Wanna walk with me and tell me about it?"

My big brown eyes meet hers. "No."

I crawl out as Mom opens the front door again. "There you are you little ————! Get to school!" she screams, yanking my arm and pushing the back of my head to make me walk. "She never listens," Mom explains to the counselor, her face and shoulders twitching. "I tell her to go to school, but she stays up too late watching television."

The attendance counselor convinces me with her consoling, soothing voice to go to school with her. She holds my hand and talks with me, smiling down at me often as we walk. The warmth of her hand feels like love passing into mine and makes me feel safe. I walk with her to make her happy and proud of me, but when she goes to her office, I wander off school property and venture down the street, past our complex, along a gravel pathway, across a large field, over a set of railroad tracks, and through another field to the park, where I play by myself.

On the weekends, I try to make friends with kids my age whose parents bring a cooler with them—a good sign they've brought food. I continually ask kids whether they want to sit with their parents to have a snack. If I'm lucky, they say yes and share with me. I'm not like the other kids on the playground or in the wading pool. I don't have parents with me. And, as usual, I'm alone. Moms and Dads slather their kids in sunscreen before letting them in the water. My skin is red and sunburned, with huge, bubbling water blisters on my shoulders and back.

I see a pig-tailed brunette fall on the playground and run crying toward the open arms of her father. *I would have been fine if I fell from that height*, I think to myself. Her father, who is talking with a friend, hears his daughter's cry and recognizes it instantly. He runs toward her, scoops her up, and holds her tight. I gaze intently and try to figure out their relationship. I want what I see between them, but it confuses me. His face looks just as pained as hers, as if he's just fallen too. I purposely fall right after she does. I tightly scrunch my body into a ball, holding my knee and screaming loudly. I lift my head with one eye open to see whether her dad notices me. I think maybe he'll open his arms out for me too, but he doesn't, and he continues to console his daughter.

I get up and sit on the swing set with my bare feet dangling above the dirt below me and watch, smiling, as the little girl beside me shouts with pure joy, "Do an 'under-doggy' Daddy!"

He laughs with her affectionately. "Again?"

As her father swings her high in the sky, I imagine him swinging me too, feeling as though I'm halfway to heaven. I close my eyes and soar with her in my mind, flying as free as a bird above the troubles of my life.

My imagination is abruptly interrupted when he stops the swing and tells her it's time to go home for supper. He smiles at me as he walks away, leaving me alone on my unmoving, rusted swing. I can't muster up the courage to ask whether I can go home with him to eat. I'm really hungry too.

I continue to gently sway back and forth on my swing, kicking off the ground with my right foot ever so gently. The rhythmic squeak from the rusty metal chain lulls my mind. I lean my body backward and daydream of a castle in the sky nestled among buoyant marshmallow clouds—the place I imagine I live.

I'm a princess in my own magnificent fortress, sitting on a damp, cold stone window ledge, taking in the beauty of the fuchsia evening sky. I'm in the tallest room of the tallest tower, dreaming and waiting to be rescued. The tower's view makes me feel as if I can reach out and cup the fading sun with my hands. I'm on top of the world, brimming with hope that I'll soon see him—my valiant, noble, and courageous father—riding through the clouds to deliver me from this isolation.

I dream of my father, my hero, flying across the crimson sky toward me, his cape rippling behind him in the breeze. I imagine his kind brown eyes looking right into mine as he divides the wind with his strong fist pushed out ahead of him like Superman. My father will bust through the walls keeping me captive, scoop me up, and let me ride on the tail of his cape into the horizon.

I begin to worry and become doubtful. Maybe he's gotten lost. Maybe he's tired and has fallen asleep. Maybe he's come and I didn't notice. Maybe he's given up on his search for me. I hush my fears and continue to wait.

I see a black shadow approaching my castle. "It has to be him; I just know it!" I say to myself, excitedly. Only my father can fly; there is no one else in the world like him. Everything I dream of is about to come true. I vigorously wave my left hand from side to side and shake the train of my dangling dress out the window with my right.

"No, this can't be …" A veil of darkness cocoons my father as he approaches me. He comes close enough that I can see his face under the shadow of his hood. His eyebrows furrow, and his evil smile displays drooling, jagged teeth. His beady eyes glow red and shoot lasers toward me, fracturing the ground beneath my feet. He lets out a roaring, terrifying laugh as he flies over me and keeps going. My shrieks of terror radiate as the walls and the stone beneath my feet begin to crack. My tower of isolation is crumbling.

Daddy, don't leave me here.

The fantastical world I created crashes to the ground, and once again I am sitting in the fragments of my dreams. *I'm such a fool.* I jump off the swing with tears in my eyes and walk back to our housing complex.

I am determined to find my way without my father. My dream has died, but I will live.

I want to be back in my porch box anyway, my place of refuge.

It's where I run to be alone when Mom or her abusers get mad or aggressive with me. It's where I sit on the cold cement in the middle of the night, with my back resting against the red brick wall of our house, and dream.

I look out to the soothing orange glow of the parking lot lights as my stomach aches and grumbles for food. I assume my familiar position of comfort, resting my tear-stained face against my knees, hugging them close to my chest. I dream of Rachel. I dream of being loved. I dream of being clean. I dream of having a father and being wanted.

* * *

In January 1991, the vice principal from my school, Warden Avenue, sends a notice to the CCAS stating that Mom's children are not attending school. They warn them that if we do not attend, the school social worker will press truancy charges. They deliver the notice to Mom and explain what they mean.

In February 1992, the vice principal again tells the society workers we still aren't attending school. Again, they bring Mom paperwork and explain what it means. At the end of the school year, in late June, professionals hold a case conference to strategize a plan between our family, the school, and the society. The society worker tells everyone the children continue to be neglected but says that until the society can prove it, they cannot apprehend us. The school attendance counselor speaks up about our lack of attendance. She is informed that poor attendance is not grounds for CCAS involvement. She's told to continue documenting her worries and to notify CCAS if she finds other things to complain about.

In 1994, at the end of the school year, the society receives yet another complaint from our vice principal stating we aren't attending school. He tells them we're constantly dirty and begging our neighbors for food. He and his colleagues are concerned about our clothing and hygiene. We smell so bad the principal sends us home from school. He tells them my shoes are very worn, buttons are missing from my shirt, and I smell like urine. The attendance counselor, who picks me up from my house sometimes, tells the principal we're dumping clothes onto the streets, and a maintenance employee complains about human waste all over our house.

In September 1994, the beginning of what's supposed to be my third-grade year, the society receives a report saying our unit is filthy and we're covered in feces, bruises, and open sores. Two days later, a health specialist and society worker knocks on our door and asks to speak with Mom. I can hear them expressing their concerns about how filthy our place is and complaining about the hundreds of cockroaches in the entryway. I sprint past them and take off running down the street before they try to catch me and send me to school.

The public school is a stone's throw from our complex. I hate going to school because I smell like sewage, but I'm eight years old and really want to make some friends. I decide to give it a try.

I try to focus, but I'm distracted by the adult-sized lice enjoying their daily buffet of my scalp. They're having a neighborhood party on my head, and my scratching complaints don't make them stop. The ones that get lost venture down my forehead toward my nose. I cross my eyes and focus on them, and I then kill them with a quick pinch and throw them on the ground, hoping my classmates won't notice. Instead, they scream to our teacher about my disgusting hair. I feel like a red-faced, flea-riddled mutt. My classmates stay far away from me and make it very clear they will not be my friends. Once again I'm sent home from school with nothing but the lice on my head, the only living things willing to get close to me. No one seems to care that I don't belong.

I wish I could like going to school. I feel sorry for myself for not having any friends, being sent home because of how dirty and stinky I am, and for the bugs in my hair. I see my classmates plugging their noses, pointing, and laughing at me from across the room. My lingering stench makes being my friend unbearable. I don't fit in, and I know it. But my teacher is wrong; I don't like being independent. I determine that when I'm older, I'm going to be a great friend to many.

I wonder how well the other students would focus if they were always hungry. My brain feels dry and defective, and I'm lethargic and tired. I can't sit still like the other kids in class. Sitting still has never been required of me before. I don't know how to behave here, and I don't care to learn. I can't control my infected bladder, let alone my temper.

I sway from side to side as I sing to myself. My teacher tells me to be quiet with her pointer finger over her mouth. When I continue singing, she firmly says, "Zip your lips, and throw away the key." She then pinches her pointer finger and thumb together in front of her mouth, gives it a twist, and pretends to toss something over her shoulder. *What a weirdo.* What does that even mean? I can barely hear what she says because my ears are infected again. I realize I'm partially deaf and learn to read the teacher's lips when she talks to me.

The CCAS has years and years of reports about the neglect we face daily. We starve and beg for food. We're constantly covered in urine and our own human waste. We have no clean clothes and are afflicted with bruises and open sores. We are barbarians without boundaries, and our mother is addicted to men. Our home is infested with mice, rodents, and cockroaches. Our heads are infested with lice. I will start grade four next year, and I've rarely been to school.

CHAPTER FIVE

Unruly Behavior (1991–1995)

The Society worker pointed out that the ongoing neglect continued to be an issue, but the children were ordered to return home in July 1991 and unless the Society could prove the care had deteriorated, the Society could not apprehend the children.

—CCAS report, June 1992

Life in the parking lot complex gets even wilder as Mom's children grow older. I'm six years old and more stubborn than ever. My siblings and I do what we want when we want, and we don't abide by social norms. I laugh until my stomach hurts when my brothers pull their pants down and squat to poop into empty pizza boxes. My brothers deliver them to the neighbors' porch across the parking lot, ring their doorbell, and run back toward us to hide. We wait for the victims to open the door and look around with confused "I didn't order pizza" looks on their faces. They open the lid slowly and reveal a steaming fresh pile of human dung. When they realize what it is, they immediately drop it and spill it on the ground. They cough and gag, wave their fists, and cuss loud, angry words to the wind. They make sure the entire complex knows how angry they are. We are on our backs, holding our stomachs and howling with laughter.

On the days we skip school, we go to the corner variety store and plan out how we're going to steal food without John, the owner, knowing. My brothers distract him at the front counter and make him count out one-cent candies we can't afford, while Ellie and I stuff our shirts and pants with handfuls of candy from the open boxes in the aisles. Then we go hang out in the forest to eat our snacks. I smoke unfinished cigarettes we find on the ground. I take a puff and choke and cough, then laugh and inhale again. I'm smoking, drinking, cussing, and constantly getting hurt. We do whatever we want. If we don't want to go to school, we don't go. Mom would have to stop her show and chase us to get us to go, but we're quick and stubborn, and she's lazy.

We make pee bombs by urinating into empty bottles and throwing them out the window at people passing by on the sidewalk. We cut a child and feel bad, but it doesn't stop us. When the lid is open and the bottle lands the right way, it creates an epic explosion.

We have legendary battles with Mom's fried sliced potatoes and onions. We take an entire bottle of ketchup and dunk the potatoes until all we see is ketchup and no potatoes. We draw a line on the floor and stand shoulder to shoulder. Every player takes aim and hopes to land a potato on its flat side against the wall. We gently swing our arms up and down twice for aiming practice while ketchup drips all over the floor. Ready … Aim … Fire! The one whose potato slaps the wall and slides down the longest is the winner. The room looks like a crime scene. Without cleaning a single thing, we leave the room and look for the next fun thing to do, but not before wiping our hands on anything within reach.

Mom's inattentiveness results in a devastating accident for my four-year-old little sister, Ellie. She's a small, delicate girl who doesn't talk much and does whatever is asked of her. She holds her emotions deep inside and is often seen sitting deep in thought with her hands folded neatly in her lap while she takes in her surroundings. She has the chubbiness of a toddler on the brink of a growth spurt, with thin and wispy dirty blonde hair that flies up in its entirety with a simple gentle breeze. Her full cheeks make her eyes disappear every time she smiles. She is my best friend and the cutest kid I know.

At four years old, Ellie knows that if she wants to eat, she needs to battle the mice and roaches and help herself. She's unattended and wanders her way into the kitchen, looking for a snack, but is too small to see over the counter. She pulls the oven door down toward the ground, not knowing Mom is boiling a big pot of water up top, and places her knee onto it to climb up. Her bit of weight causes the entire stove and boiling pot of water to come tumbling down on top of her little body. The thunderous sound of crashing metal follows Ellie's tortured scream. Mom and I run into the kitchen to see what happened. My best friend is trapped beneath the stove, desperately crying for help in the most agonizing screech I've ever heard her make. I hold my breath then release it as I wail for my sister.

"Ellie!" I scream. "Oh, my God!" I curse repeatedly. "Is she going to die?" I ask Mom.

Mom pulls her body out from underneath the stove and away from the puddle of dirty boiled water on the floor. I fall to my sister's side and notice thick blisters that are growing from her leg and filling with fluid. I'm scared and don't know what to do. I stroke her matted hair and cry over her body as she clings to me and Mom, who's panicking and calling for an ambulance. The paramedics arrive quickly and strap her body onto a long stretcher. She looks so small. They lift her into the back of the ambulance and close the doors. They won't let me go with her. I cry hysterically and chase the ambulance down the road. I'm worried my worst nightmare will come true—that the CCAS will take her from the hospital and that I'll never see her again. I've lost too many people who have left and never come back.

After a month alone in the hospital, Ellie returns, and I am filled with relief.

"I'm so glad you're back, Ellie." I squeeze her hard. "I thought I'd never see you again."

Ellie and I love playing in our backyard together. Our unit is the closest to the street and has a tall brick wall on the north side of our small yard that keeps lurking people on the sidewalk from seeing us. All the backyards down our units' row are divided with chain-link fences, and a narrow concrete path separates our backyards from the back neighbors' backyards. Everyone can see what his or her neighbors are doing outside.

One game we like to play against each other is called the naked race, where we streak through the backyard in our birthday suits, racing from the house to the back fence. One hand has to be on the house before I give the go-ahead. I shout "Ready? Steady, *bap!*" imitating a gunshot. I'm older than Ellie, so I have the privilege of saying when to go. The naked race is always more fun when it's raining, and even better when it pours. We slip and slide like pigs in mud, laughing and carrying on until the only white spots on our entire bodies are our eyeballs. The goggling eyes leering at us from our neighbors' back windows don't bother us. As far as we're concerned, we have an audience to perform for.

As soon as lightning strikes, we run inside. We jump and wrestle with each other on the urine-stained mattresses Mom has thrown down the steps, and we then run upstairs to pollute the house with our filthy, rancid-smelling bodies.

We often beg our neighbors for food, sometimes even in the middle of the night. I know it annoys them when we ask, but we beg only when we're absolutely starving. If no one answers the door, we return home to our soiled mattresses with aching stomachs that moan like a choir of bullfrogs in the night. When one of our stomachs growls louder and longer than another, we laugh in amazement at the new record. I love being together with my siblings in the same room. It brings me comfort and makes me feel safe.

Iram, who lives to the right of us, is always cooking delicious food. When she cooks, aromas dance through the air and make our mouths water. I crave whatever she's cooking. She tells us it's our mother's job to feed us. When Iram can, she shares with us.

Alvita, who lives a few doors down from us, is outside sweeping her porch in her tank top with her right elbow high as she motions her broom back and forth.

"You could sweep the whole sidewalk with your armpit hair," I laugh. "It looks like you're smuggling upside-down troll dolls in your pits!"

"You need a butt whupping today, little girl?" She has a serious look on her face, but I know she's teasing me.

"Let me get a pair of scissors. I'll cut it off for you." I make snipping motions with my fingers and giggle.

She hits me hard on the rear end with her broom. "You will do no such thing, child. Now leave me alone before I whup you good!"

I like her. Gatherings outside of her house happen often. Reggae music plays loudly, bodies move to the rhythm of the beats, food is passed around, and the sound of laughter echoes in the air. I join in and swing my hips while knocking every skinny bone in my body together. I have no idea whether the words in the songs are in English or not, but I sing along without a care in the world of being wrong. I am a tolerated uninvited guest, and I'm okay with that.

Mom waits every month for her welfare check to come in and when it does, she immediately cashes it. Rachel isn't around to take care of Mom's finances now, and I'm too young to know how. Mom and we kids feel rich and live spoiled for an entire week. We order pizza or Chinese takeout or pay for a taxi and get fast food downtown. We order whatever we want and more. We take trips to an amusement park called Center Island in downtown Toronto and sometimes go to the zoo. The high of luxury living doesn't last long. The consequence of our fun is being hungry for the rest of the month, relying heavily on food banks and the generosity of others.

I am either desensitized to the deaths in my community or I'm too young to understand murder. I'm more scared of Mom's candles blowing out in the living room than I am about the crime happening in our community. I get excited when the camera crews and reporters show up outside our house. I love looking at the reporter's fancy clothes that hug her stiff body as she talks very seriously into the spongy microphone. I dance in front of the yellow caution tape, doing the moonwalk as I mimic her hand gestures and facial expressions behind her back. I interrupt and challenge her attention. The reporter and cameraman get so frustrated with me that they promise to interview me on camera if I stop interrupting. After their segment, they point the camera toward me. I let my personality shine while they ask questions. I'm good at getting what I want.

There's a group of boys, mostly between the ages of nine and twelve years old, that cluster together and wander the streets with scrap wood weapons that resemble baseball bats. They hammer long, pointy nails through the ends of the wood to increase fear and do extra damage to their enemies. We know to drop whatever it is we're doing and book it home as fast as we can when they pass our house.

Cataraqui, the subdivision across the road, has been named "Block 13" by the Toronto Community Housing Corporation. It's full of gun violence, gangs, and drugs. It's crime-ridden, scary, and dangerous. Cataraqui Park is in a grassy valley with a neglected forest area full of garbage and debris—perfect for crime. Up the hill of Cataraqui is the field attached to our school, Warden Avenue. We play on Cataraqui's playground unsupervised all the time.

Rimmy is a teenage girl who lives with her elderly grandmother across the road from us. Her small house sits on the other side of our schoolyard fence. She's a lot older than I am and convinces me we're friends. She makes me stand against the red brick wall of our unit, then places her hands around my neck and adds pressure until I almost faint. Right before I lose consciousness, she releases her grip from my neck so I can feel the cool, tingling rush of blood as it enters my head again. She assures me that if I faint, I won't die. I don't want to die. She's extremely friendly with my older brothers and shows me attention. She invites me over to her place for lunch and tells me her grandma is going to make us soup. Instead of the promise of food, she brings me downstairs and pushes me onto the small navy couch and takes advantage of my young body the same way men do to mom's when they come to our house at night. I don't like it. I don't want to see Rimmy anymore. I refuse to go over to her house when she invites me.

Mom is getting attention too, but not the good kind. Gloria, Mom's terrorizing neighbor, kicked her own husband down the stairs, which led to him being hospitalized for two months. After his hospital stay, he asks Mom whether he can come and live with us instead of returning home to his deranged wife. Mom tells him no because she doesn't want Gloria mad at her. When Gloria finds out her husband asked to stay with us, she sends two of her friends and two teenagers to our house, and they beat Mom to a pulp in front of us. Gloria stands there smiling as she watches her friends grab fistfuls of Mom's hair, kick her in the ribs, and punch her in the face repeatedly. I try to pull them off her, but they shove me to the ground too. I don't know how to help Mom. My heart is broken, and my body is enraged. Mom is traumatized by the beating and wants out of Housing as soon as possible. When her monthly check comes in, we are in a taxi right away, heading toward the Brampton area to stay in a run-down one-room motel.

CHAPTER SIX

Women's Shelters, Motels, And Cain (1995)

C.C.A.S has been involved for 12 years, off and on for neglect concerns. They are at the point where they are ready to close the case - no abuse - simply neglect...

—CCAS reports, February 1995

It was noted that past efforts had failed to improve the home situation. The file remained open for a short time due to the increasing number of professionals expressing their concerns.

—CCAS report, 1995

Over four-month period numerous complaints were received. Most were not investigated since the previous concerns had been investigated.

—CCAS report, 1995

I t's a freezing cold winter day in February 1995, and the manager from the Flowertown Motel in Brampton just called the Peel police service to report our family. There are seven of us living in a dumpy single motel room, which includes Mom, her five kids, and her abusive boyfriend, Cain, whom we despise. Mom is also five months pregnant with Cain's baby; he is the fifth father to her ninth child.

By my childish standards, Cain looks revolting and is completely insane. Mom apparently has a thing for the short ones, because he's little too. His eyes are gray and lifeless, and his mouth and fingers are stained orange from chain-smoking cigarettes. The top half of his head is dirty and bald, and the bottom half has long, straggly, thinning gray hair that dangles past his shoulders. He's missing his front tooth, and his leg is all chewed up from getting electrocuted. His bad leg is skinnier than his other one, and he hobbles like a pirate when he walks. The kids scream when he pulls his pant leg up, because his whole leg looks like an old, wrinkled potato.

My brothers make it difficult for Cain to throw Mom around or talk to her the way he does. My brothers are young teenagers now, and much stronger than before. They're extremely protective of Mom. They threaten Cain several times, warning him that if he ever lays a finger on Mom again, it will be over for him. Cain is frustrated and threatens to hang himself, thinking we'll beg him not to. He starts walking toward the bush across the road, and we follow him to watch. It's not the reaction he wants. He turns around, puffs his chest out, and heads back toward our motel room. My brothers aren't about to let him in our room and want him gone, away from our family forever. They end up in a fistfight in the parking lot. Blaire punches Cain square in the face with his metal skull ring, leaving a symbolic imprint of Cain's future on his forehead if he ever touches Mom again.

A police officer arrives at the motel and sees Mom's five kids playing alone outside with no coats, socks, or shoes. We haven't eaten in two days and tell the police officer we're starving. The officer listens to us as he scribbles on his notepad. He makes a referral call to the Children's Aid Society, then leaves. The next day, a society worker comes to check on us. She interviews us, and we tell her everything she needs to know. She drives Blaire to and from the food bank and brings home enough food to last a day or two. She sends the information to our family worker, who states, "CCAS has been involved with this family for twelve years, off and on, for neglect concerns. They are at the point where they are ready to close the case—no abuse, simply neglect—but it is a resistant family, and there is not enough concern to apprehend."

No abuse. Simply neglect.

There is nothing simple about being neglected.

It's 11:00 a.m. the next morning. Mom tells us we're leaving the Flowertown Motel and calls us a taxi. With only the clothes on our backs, we're off to a women's shelter. Mom and Cain are fighting constantly, and being around them is getting increasingly stressful for all of us. Mom and Cain's verbal abuse toward us is degrading and volatile. The crossfire of accusations between them is getting worse. I'm tired of it; we all are. We just want Cain to go away, to disappear forever, and leave us and our mother alone. Mom is drawn to men who provide chaos, and I don't understand why.

Being at a women's shelter means Cain is not allowed to be there with us. I feel safe and excited, but also very nervous, because Cain lingers outside the shelter building, loudly calling out Mom's name and begging her to leave her worthless children to run away with him. Mom tries numerous times to leave us in the shelter to be with him, but the staff constantly remind her she's not allowed. All Mom thinks about is being with him. Mom is angry she's being told what to do, and I feel like she resents me. The staff document Mom's verbal abuse toward us. Mom's demeaning words used to kill my soul, but now I'm numb to them. She doesn't take care of our needs and considers the shelter staff as our caretakers. We feed ourselves, and the staff bathe us. Mom has lost all interest in what we're doing and where we're going. The staff feel sorry for us, but other than reporting, they can't do anything to solve our problems. I love the way the staff care for me. They comb my hair and help brush my teeth. They dress me in fresh clothes and encourage me with their words. They listen when I speak to them, and they respond with care. They offer more when I fear I don't have enough. They tuck me into a bed with clean sheets and make me feel safe. They hold my hand and know who I am on the inside. They see the little girl within me who craves love and attention from anyone willing to give me some.

Our two weeks at the shelter are over. I don't want to leave and can feel myself begin to panic. I don't know where I'm going or whether I'll be able to find food or whether I'll starve. I get three meals a day here at the shelter, and snacks too. I don't want to beg anymore. I want the safety and predictability of routine and structure. I want to know what's going on and what's to come. I don't want to be filthy again and wandering the streets without anything to do. When we leave, Mom won't be able to afford the activities we get to do here on Wednesdays. My biggest fear right now is Cain living with us again. He ruins everything.

On March 11, Mom tells the shelter she's found a motel room in Cobourg and lets them know she's leaving.

The staff say there is no indication of physical abuse and no immediate risk indicating the need for CCAS to visit our family tonight.

On March 16, we arrive at Tom's Motel in Cobourg, ninety-five kilometers from Scarborough. Society workers are called because of complaints about our family. Cain accelerates the destruction and turmoil we go through and makes my mother absolutely insane. This, by far, is the worst of being unhoused we've experienced. Again, we are seven people stuffed in a single motel room without food, clothing, or money. Cain screams at the workers, demanding we go to a shelter where there is babysitting so he can be with other women. He accuses Mom of being with other men and says she performs sexual acts in front of her children. I roll my eyes and tell the worker, "See, this is what we have to put up with all the time."

The society workers gather the children outside to ask more questions. They ask what I think of Cain, and I tell them I hate him and that he beats our mother in front of me, whips beer cans at me, and, worse, dumps his beer over my head as if I'm worthless. I tell them I can't sleep because of the fighting.

The society workers have heard enough and tell us to pack our things because they refuse to leave us in this situation. When we arrive at the women's shelter in Peterborough, Mom is warned that if she leaves with Cain, they will take her children.

This is another shelter I enjoy being at. What I love most is Cain not being here. I think Mom has taken the warning of the staff seriously. I'm hoping she'll pay more attention to us now, but she's six months pregnant, tired, lonely, and depressed. I am brimming with excitement to be here. The shelter has daily activities, such as bowling, swimming, nature walks, movies, and game nights. The staff are cheerful. There are other kids to play with. We have clean beds to sleep in, nightly baths, clean clothes, and hot meals. It's a dream come true for me. The downfall is that the shelter will allow us to stay for only a few weeks. It isn't permanent. Nothing in my life is permanent. Joy and hope are always short-lived.

The shelter enrolls us in school for a couple weeks, and I attend a field trip to the city jail. I brag to the teachers and students, huddled in front of the jail cells in the basement, about how my dad is in jail. I've dreamed of seeing what a jail cell looks like from the inside and beg the guide to lock me in the cell by myself, and he does. It's the highlight of my trip.

During our four-month period of being unhoused, we learn that several professionals and members of the public are reporting concerns about our family to the CCAS from various jurisdictions around Ontario. Complaints and reports have come from the following institutions and people:

- Toronto Catholic Children's Aid Society
- Peel Children's Aid Society
- Northumberland Children's Aid Society
- Kawartha-Haliburton Children's Aid Society
- Toronto Police Service
- motel managers
- society workers
- family support workers
- child management workers
- family benefit workers
- Salvation Army Family Services
- a public health nurse
- our school vice principal
- our school principal
- Our school social worker

- a communications worker
- a cable television worker
- medical doctors
- a dentist
- neighbors
- several anonymous callers

The CCAS constantly reports the neglect I endure, and sometimes it feels as though they neglect me too. I want to live a better life with my family. It's such a difficult thing to explain. I don't want to live like this anymore but can't fathom the thought of being apart from the only ones I love. I can't relax. The stress from the push and pull of my feelings makes me feel as if there's a hive of angry buzzing bees swarming throughout my body with no way to exit. I pull my hair and pick my scabs. I bite my fingernails and the skin around them until my fingers bleed. I can't control my bladder and still wet the bed. My body feels out of control and full of fear. My mind operates as if there's a monster under my bed or I'm walking past a rustling bush in the middle of the night. I need rest.

It seems as if all these agencies are saying, "We've heard these complaints a million times before. They're a hopeless family. We're tired of the paperwork. Stop calling us." It feels like they've given up on our family because we're too much work. Our family is unhoused again and no longer residing in Toronto, so they close our file. I'm sure they're thankful we moved out of their jurisdiction so they don't have to put up with the annoying calls from the increasing number of professionals expressing their concerns.

We're in Peterborough now, at yet another motel. Seven of us, once again, are staying in a single room. It's a day like any other. Mom has just left to make a phone call; it's my and Ellie's turn to leave the family.

✣

CHAPTER SEVEN

Taken (April 1995)

As the family was no longer residing in Toronto, <u>the file was closed</u> in April 1995.

—CCAS report, 1995

Mom takes me and Ellie out of our motel room to stand outside. Mom's brother, Steve, and his wife, Lisa, pull into the parking lot. I didn't know they were visiting today.

Mom looks down at me and Ellie and says, "You girls are going to live with them now." She points toward their car. "You can't stay here with me anymore. They're going to take you to live with them."

"You called them to take us?" My body remembers the agonizing battle I fought as a three-year-old being given away by Mom. I cross my arms and squeeze my ribs to hold myself. "I thought you were ordering pizza!" *This is some cruel joke. Maybe she's angry about something I did.* "You told us you'd never let anyone take us!" I remind her. "You lied!" I accuse her. Then, hoping I'm wrong, I ask, "Are you lying to me?"

"No. You're leaving with them."

"I'm not going anywhere with them. You can't make me go. I'm staying here with you and Rosie, Ellie, and Blaire and Dylan." Lisa approaches us. *Run, Lainie.* Panic rushes through my brain as if through a floodgate, and fear is pounding on my chest. I realize Mom is being serious. Everything I know is coming to an end. My blood rushes to my face like magma in a volcano waiting to erupt and makes my skin feel as if it's burning. My body tightens, and my fists close. I stand taller and puff out my chest. When I finally inhale, I strengthen my voice and scream in horror, "I'm not going with them! Mom! What have you done? You don't want me again?" I try to bargain with her. "I'll be better, Mom, I promise! *Mom!* Please! Don't do this! Don't you love me?"

"Yes, I love both of you children," she says calmly. "You can't live without a home anymore."

"Yes, I can! I can, Mom." I plead. Tears gather in the corners of my eyes and begin to fall down my face. "I don't want to go! Tell them to go back home!"

I grab Ellie's hand and hide her behind Mom's back. I peek around her waist. Everything feels different. I squeeze my little sister's hand even tighter and pull her closer to my body. Adrenaline bubbles inside, and my heart races. I grab a fistful of Ellie's shirt and bunch it up tightly behind her back. I'm ready to carry her like a baton in a relay. If I hear even a single word out of Steve and Lisa's mouths that triggers panic, I'll begin my freedom sprint with Ellie flailing in the wind like a rag doll. They're getting closer. I prepare my body to fight. I have almost nine years' experience protecting myself. I'm stubborn, and I'm fast.

"If you love us, then stop them!" I can barely breathe from screaming so hard and crying. My chest is pumping up and down, and my ribs hurt.

"*Help me! Mom!*" I beg.

"It's okay, Lainie," Lisa says. "I'm not going to hurt you." Lisa reaches toward me, but I push her hand away and curse at her. "Don't touch me! *No!* I'm not going anywhere with you. I'm not living with you, and I'm *not* getting in your car!"

Steve reaches for me, and I flail and twist my body to break his grip on me. My shirt is up to my neck, but I release myself from his grip. I'm red all over my body and take off sprinting to make a clean getaway.

"Lainie! Be careful of the road!" Lisa yells. Ellie can't keep up with me; she's little, and her legs are short. She willingly takes Lisa's hand and walks to their car. She isn't scared because she doesn't understand what's happening. I do. I make the split-second decision to leave Ellie behind, vowing to find a way to rescue her later. I want to run for miles. *But Ellie ... I don't know what to do. They're putting her into their car. No. I can't let them take her.* I scream at Ellie to get out of the car and run to try and save her. Steve grabs me and forcefully puts me into the car too. They restrain me with a seatbelt, but I take it off and try to jump out. I try repeatedly but fail. Lisa has her legs wrapped around mine and her arms squeezed tightly around my chest, locking my body. Steve quickly jumps into the front seat and starts the car. He rolls down the window and apologizes to Mom that it has to be this way. I'm still screaming for Mom, who's not fighting for me at all. I flail my body to escape Lisa's grip. I bite, kick, and scream every profane word I know, which is a lot. It's a fight for survival, and I will not back down. I continue to contort my body to get away from her grip, but Lisa's stronger than I am.

Mom's just standing there in her typical slouched posture, waving at us. Her face is expressionless, which is frustrating. I want to know what she's thinking and feeling. I wish she would make it obvious. I want her to run after me or make some sort of effort to show she doesn't want me to go. But she doesn't. Mom and my siblings are getting smaller and smaller, and we're getting farther and farther away. I scream, red-faced in anguish. I want to make it clear that all this is against my will. I want Mom to change her mind.

How can Mom say she loves me and then give me away? How could she do something so terrible if it were true? It doesn't make sense. I don't care about not having a home. My home is with her and my family. Mom is easily persuaded by men, and I'm almost positive Cain convinced her to choose him over us. He's always telling us how much he hates having us around.

Mom, this is the third time you've given me away. Even if you don't fight for me, I'll always fight for you. I want to stay. You're my home.

I determine I'll make them turn this car around. The rage within me explodes, and I become an eight-year-old Hulk. I kick the driver's seat repeatedly. I bash the back of Steve's head with a loose hand whenever it escapes his wife's restraint. I dig my bum bone into his wife's leg and use my elbow to dig into her side. I'm hyperventilating, trying to break free of Lisa's grip so I can open the door latch and jump out of the car. I feel like a fish resisting the pull of the Thompsons' line, which has hooked my mouth and silenced me. I've been reeled to shore against my will and pulled from the murky waters of my home. I am suffocating. They expect me to live on land, but I don't know how to breathe their air.

My tantrums don't affect Ellie. She's seen them plenty of times before. She's sitting quietly, looking out the window toward the sunset off the highway; it is the most beautiful display of color I have ever seen in my life. Lisa begins telling me a story: "A red sky at night is a sailor's delight. That means it's going to be a beautiful day tomorrow. A red sky in the morning is a sailor's warning, meaning you can expect bad weather the next day."

My little body has given up its fight. My soul has died. I lay my head back in exhaustion. The crimson sky is reflecting a devilish red color across Lisa's face, but I also see the sun in her eyes. I wonder who she is. My eyelids are heavy; everything feels heavy. My body sinks into Lisa's lap as she wraps me in an embrace and slowly sings "Yes, Jesus Loves Me."

I didn't get to say good-bye to my family. I feel abandoned and betrayed, rejected and alone. The woman I loved and trusted the most just gave me away for the third and final time. Mom broke her vow to me when she promised me forever, and now I will never live with her again. Being stolen from my family was the most traumatic thing I've ever experienced, and it has rewired my brain forever. The emptiness in my heart that yearns for Mom will never be filled by another. My life will never be the same as it was. I'll hold tight to the lie that screams, "If my own mother doesn't want me, then no one else will either." I do not want to feel rejected or abandoned again. I resolve that from now on I'll run away when things get hard. I'll prevent people from getting close to me, because learning to trust again will be too hard. I won't get close to others if they're going to leave me too.

CHAPTER EIGHT

Getting Used to Different

Steve pulls into his long laneway, puts the car in park, and opens his door. Lisa gently shakes us awake. "We're here, girls," she says, slowly lifting our heavy heads off her. I'm disappointed in myself for not staying awake to remember the way back to Mom. I need to know she's okay. I squint my eyes as I look up. The car's interior lights are shining in my eyes, a soft glow amid the darkness of the night. I stretch my body and yawn. Half-asleep and confused, I stumble out of the car and follow Steve and Lisa into their small beige cottage-style house.

We open the front door and enter the landing area. There's a small closet with a folding door to the left, and a larger space to the right with several pairs of shoes all neatly lined up in rows. Up a single step from the landing is a family room with a large glass patio door that leads to the raised back deck and a large yard. "I'll show you the backyard tomorrow when there's daylight," Lisa says. "The back deck overlooks an acre of open space for you to run and play. There's also a tire swing you'll love and a small, forested area along the back property line waiting for adventure." To the left of the family room, on the west side of the house, is a tiny office they've converted into the bedroom I'll be sharing with Ellie. Beside our bedroom, on the south side of the house, is Steve and Lisa's bedroom. Our four cousins sleep on the east side of the house, and the single bathroom is between their bedrooms. The living room, kitchen, laundry room, and family room fill the spaces in between.

The laminate floors are a light cream color with a darker brown design throughout. The bottom half of the walls have thin, dark sheets of wood paneling nailed to them, and above is a light-brown wallpaper with various nature-themed images. The artwork and furniture throughout the house are minimal. Nothing I see reflects little girls. This small four-bedroom house now holds six kids, two adults, a Dalmatian dog, and a Siamese cat. The home is small and simple but somehow feels spacious.

Lisa immediately directs us to the washroom and prepares a warm bath before bed.

"I know how to make a bath for us," I say matter-of-factly, "so we don't get burnt."

"I'm sure you do," Lisa replies as she continues to check the temperature of the running water with her wiggling fingers. I help Ellie undress first, then I undress myself and hop into the bath. We have no shame in being naked in front of strangers. Lisa lathers our hair with an awful-smelling tea-tree oil shampoo that stings my scalp. I look down at my bruised, skinny legs. We are filthy from head to toe. Our matted hair is full of crawling lice, and our skin and clothes smell of urine. After we dry off, Lisa hands each of us an ankle-length nightgown made of flannel. I don't wear pajamas with Mom. The necks, sleeves, and bottoms of the dresses have ruffles on them. Ellie and I look like little old ladies.

Lisa leads us to our bedroom. I stop abruptly in front of its brown door, glaring at the brass-colored doorknob. "You can go in, Lainie," Lisa says. I don't move. She reaches for the handle and swings the door open. I grab hold of both sides of the door frame for leverage in case she tries to push me in. I'm not ready. I look down at the faded brass transition strip on the floor and beg my feet to move forward. My brain alerts me of past trauma and screams at me not to enter. Ellie walks in under my arms. I grab her chest and pull her toward me, releasing my grip from the door frame. Without touching me, Lisa walks past me and stands in the center of the room. "This is it," she says, throwing her arms out and dropping them back down. I feel better knowing that she isn't standing behind me anymore.

I can see everything in this tiny room from the doorway. There are two plastic brown-paneled closet doors on sliding tracks directly in front of me. To the right of the closet is a small window facing the brick wall of the neighbors' house. The single bed I'll be sharing with Ellie is on the north side of the bedroom and barely fits between the two walls. There's a white dresser with six drawers; three on the left for me, and three on the right for Ellie, which leaves a small empty space on the floor where Lisa is standing. I don't mind the small room. I'm just happy Ellie is sharing it with me.

Ellie and I crawl into bed. I wrap my right arm over her stomach and pull her close to my body. Lisa kneels beside the bed and starts talking out loud to "Dear God." She then proceeds to talk to this man about me and my sister. I look around the room to see who she's talking to. Mom spoke to the candles and weird things happened. I listen, trying not to be scared, because she's speaking nicely to him about us. Before closing the door, Lisa tells us it's time to be quiet and go to sleep. Ellie and I lie in our bed, staring at the ceiling. I want to know when Mom is coming back to get us or when the Thompsons are going to bring us to her. This room doesn't feel right. It certainly doesn't smell familiar, and the bed feels uncomfortable. Lisa has put a thick plastic cover around the mattress, which makes it feel hard and crinkly. My siblings and I usually sleep on soiled mattresses or on piles of dirty clothes, but now we're lying in a neatly made-up bed between clean, fresh-smelling sheets with a thick blanket on top for extra warmth.

I rub my hands up and down my bruised arms to comfort myself. Fresh flashbacks of my arms being torn from Mom's legs are unforgiving and tormenting. My body physically hurts. My sore and aching muscles are a physical reminder that what happened today was real. My throat burns from screaming, my eyes are tired and swollen from crying, and my heart—my heart hurts the most. Why didn't Mom fight for us?

Ellie turns her body to face me and looks deeply into my eyes. I take hold of her hands and pull her close to my body. We touch our foreheads together and lower our chins toward our chests. Ellie's little shoulders begin to shake as she sobs. "I'm afraid, Lainie." I hold her tighter and wipe her cheek with my ruffled sleeve. "Just breathe with me, okay?" The soft glow of the moon shines across her small face. Her wet, glassy eyes sparkle like a diamond sky at night, dropping its fallen stars down the bridge of her nose and onto our bedsheets.

This isn't right. We don't belong here.

Ellie's breaths become deeper and longer. Her body finally submits to exhaustion, and she drifts into a deep slumber. I brush her thin hair behind her ear with my fingertips and weep uncontrollably. I weep for our mother. I weep for my missing siblings. I weep for Ellie. I can hardly breathe. Still holding tightly to Ellie's hands, I kiss her forehead and whisper softly, "I'm afraid too, Ellie. We'll always be together. I promise."

The night has stolen my shadow, and I feel lonelier than ever before. I'm headed toward darkness whether I like it or not. I feel like an unlovable, bad girl, as if I did something terribly wrong not to deserve my mother's love anymore, and as if I earned the punishment of being sent away and all of this is my fault. I've been the oldest girl living with Mom for the last five years. She still needs me. My mind is spinning trying to figure out the mistakes I caused to make Mom get rid of me. I don't know what I did, and it makes me feel empty, confused, and betrayed. If it was my fault, that's one thing, but I know Ellie didn't do anything to deserve this. Knowing her heart is hurting makes the pain I feel inside even worse.

Our curtainless window welcomes the morning light into our bedroom. I open my eyes to see Ellie still sleeping peacefully beside me. I take in all her beautiful features: her tiny pursed lips; her thin, wispy hair; her chubby cheeks; and her pointed little ears. We've survived so much together. I've slept all through the night and still feel tired. Yesterday was exhausting. I sit up in our bed and quickly realize I'm in a puddle of my own urine. Normally I wouldn't care, but this isn't my house. I'm almost nine years old, and I still pee the bed every night.

Lisa's gonna be mad at me. I don't want the door to open and have my bad habit revealed in front of the family. I carefully get out of bed and stand in the small empty space on the floor. I pinch my nightgown and pull it far away from my body. I look out the window, up past the roof of our neighbor's house, and take in the beauty of the morning sky. I wonder if my siblings are up yet. I wonder whether Mom has changed her mind and realized she's made a terrible mistake.

I let out a yelp when Lisa knocks on the door and wakes Ellie.

"Good morning, girls. How'd you sleep?"

Lisa looks at my dress stretched far from my body. I tell her in language she doesn't approve of that I wet the bed.

"You peed the bed, you mean," she corrects me immediately.

"'I didn't even say a bad word!" I laugh in disbelief.

"We don't talk like that here. You'll have to strip the bed."

"I'm not stripping."

"Take the sheets off and put them in the laundry," she explains.

"I don't do that ..."

"You'll do it from now on. Every time you wet the bed; you'll change your own sheets. I'll show you how this time, but next time, it'll be your responsibility," she says calmly.

Lisa helps Ellie out of the bed and asks her to lift her arms to take her nightgown off. I step in front of her. "I'll do it." I slip it above her head and toss it by the door, then do the same for myself. I apologize to Ellie for peeing on her and pull her in for a hug. I keep my arm around her chubby naked frame while Lisa goes to get us soapy cloths to wipe our bodies down. Once we're clean, she hands us a fresh set of clothes from our closet, and we proudly put them on. She teaches me how to strip the sheets by crawling onto the mattress and pulling the sheets from its four corners. I laugh and tell her it sounds as if she's rolling on a bag of chips. She sprays and wipes the plastic cover and remakes the bed. She picks up the bunched-up pile of dirty bedding, tells us to pick up our nightgowns by the door, and leads us to the laundry room to show us how the washing machine works and how to operate the dials. I think the machine is so fascinating; Mom washed our clothes in the bathtub. I love the smell of the detergent she puts in. I love the bubbles it's creating. I love holding my hand under the water as it pours into the drum. Mostly, I love that my sheets and pajamas will smell clean.

Lisa pulls a spare set of sheets from the linen closet and shows me how to put them on the bed.

Night after night, I knock on Lisa's door, calling for her to help me change the sheets, but she won't answer me. I have to change the bed on my own without waking her. I wake Ellie every night to help her change into dry pajamas. I feel terrible that she has to share a bed with me, but there's nowhere else I'd rather her sleep. She sits on the floor half-asleep, her head bobbing as she waits for me to strip the bed, wipe the plastic cover, run the washing machine, and remake the bed with fresh sheets. Steve and Lisa eventually get us a small white metal bunk bed. We are thrilled about our new sleeping arrangements but miss falling asleep together. Some nights Ellie sneaks down to sleep with me, but only if I promise not to pee on her. I tell her I'll try my best, but I fail. Ellie quickly gets used to sleeping on the top bunk alone.

I've been a bedwetter my whole life. It didn't matter so much when I was with Mom, but at the Thompsons', it's a problem I have to fix. I have terrifying recurring nightmares that debilitate me and paralyze my body. It's usually on those nights I wet the bed. I'm never safe in my dreams. They scare me. I want it to stop, but it's beyond my control. I don't want to smell like urine anymore. Lisa doesn't allow me to drink liquids after supper, and I use the washroom before bed, but still, it doesn't work.

Lisa prays with me about my future husband before bed. I close my eyes during her prayer but smile from ear to ear the whole time. She prays for God to keep my sweetheart safe and pure; I think this means he'll be clean and take lots of showers. I imagine our first kiss and think that I'll be the only girlfriend he'll ever have and that as soon as our eyes meet, we'll run into each other's arms knowing we waited our whole young lives for each other. I dream of the boy I've created in my mind during the nights and fantasize about him during the day too. What does he like to do for fun? What does his laugh sound like? Will he love me even though I still wet the bed?

I imagine the bedpost on the bottom bunk is the husband I've been praying for. I get carried away sometimes, I admit. I passionately kiss the cold metal, tongue and all, stopping occasionally to laugh at its funny joke. I twist my hair with my fingers while I smack my lips together, pretending to chew gum. I roll my eyes when it teases me. I give the post a wink and laugh again, scrunching my nose up to show all my teeth. I stare at it until my eyes grow tired and heavy, then kiss it again and wish it a good night. Ellie hears sloppy kissing sounds from the top bunk and screams out loud to Lisa that I'm kissing the bedpost again. I bury my head under the covers in humiliation but know my bedpost understands that our love is so strong it makes others jealous sometimes.

We gather every morning at the breakfast table with the Thompsons' four boys. It feels unusual to eat together, because that happened in my family only when we ate fast food together in a restaurant. Lisa toasts thick slices of homemade bread and spreads butter and homemade strawberry jam across them. The smell of fresh bread has me salivating. She serves her two youngest boys first, then Ellie, me, and her oldest two boys. I can barely contain my excitement, and I'm growing impatient. When she finally places the bread in front of me, I devour four huge bites right in a row. I look like a full-cheeked squirrel chewing with my mouth open. I have never tasted such fresh and fluffy bread before. "We pray before we eat, Lainie," Lisa says as she lowers my hands from my mouth. I continue to shove the bread into my mouth during her prayer.

"Next time, you'll wait until the prayer is finished before you eat," she says firmly.

"I want more," I say.

"You've had enough now."

"No, I haven't!" I scream. "Give me more! It's so good. I'm so hungry. Please."

"You'll have to wait until lunch. Go sit on the floor by the couch. I'm going to look through your hair." She prompts me with her finger, pointing down to the carpet.

I don't want to sit. I want more food. What if there isn't enough later? What if I have to wait to eat until tomorrow? What if everyone else takes a lot and there isn't enough left for me? I need there to be enough for me. I continue to argue and throw profane words at Lisa like slaps to the face. She marches me to my room and shuts the door.

I kick it from behind. "I hate you!" I holler from behind the door. "I don't want to be with you ————s anyway!"

I sit on the edge of my mattress, looking down at my half-bitten-off fingernails. *Mom … Rosie … my brothers …* I'm drowning in sorrow and don't know what to do to make myself feel better. I don't know how to get back to Mom. I drop to my knees on the floor and cover my face. I grieve for my mother, my brothers, and my sisters.

"*I hate it here!*" I cry out, making sure Lisa hears me. I begin to rock my body back and forth to try to soothe myself. I scream forceful, pulsing cries of anguish until I release every bit of air from my lungs. "I just want to go home … please, just let me go home!" I inhale as if my chest is stealing air, emitting a dry, screeching, hiccup-like noise that scratches my throat and makes me cough.

"Are you quite done yet, Lainie?" Lisa asks as she opens the door.

"I want to go home!" I snap back.

"This is your home right now. Your mom is sick and can't take care of you."

"Yes she can! And she's not sick. Take me back, *now!*" I demand. Why is she saying my mom is sick? She doesn't even have a cough. I would know whether she was sick or not. I don't believe her. Mom was perfectly fine when I saw her last. "I don't want to be here. Don't you understand? I want to be with my mom and family."

"We are your family too, Lainie," she says.

"You're not my mother," I say through clenched teeth. "I don't want you." I miss the chaos of my life. I miss being able to do whatever I want, such as eating more than a single piece of toast, without anyone telling me no.

"When you've finished carrying on in here, you can come out and sit by the couch like I've asked," she says sternly. "I'm ready to go through your hair."

I'm ready to sit in this room all day, and I want to, but I hate being in a room with a closed door, and I need to see whether Ellie is okay. I look out the bedroom window one more time and wish for my mom. I consider that maybe the "Dear God" Lisa prays to will bring me back to my family. I wipe my tears with my sleeve and slowly walk to the living room carpet. I sit down to rest my back against the couch and wait for Lisa, who's headed toward me with the stinky tea tree oil mixture from the bathroom. I sit between her knees while she pours the cold, stinging liquid all over my scalp; I can almost hear the lice screaming. For the next three hours, I sit numb in the bum, with my head and neck being moved in every direction as if I am a salon mannequin. Lisa picks through my hair like a baboon, pulling bugs and eggs from almost every strand of hair attached to my scalp. She passes me a paper towel and begins to swipe her small-toothed comb across it. Crawling black lice are stumbling around and struggling to turn themselves over from being upside down. I let them crawl around for a bit, then squish them in the towel between my fingertips so I can feel them explode. I am both shocked and amazed every time she hands me a crawling bug. Lisa's boys are standing at a distance, glancing quickly from my head to their mom's face, expecting her to have the same reaction they do, but she doesn't. They repeatedly gasp in disbelief, cover their mouths and scream, "Ew! Disgusting!" I don't know what all their fuss is about, but I chuckle at their panicked, grossed-out reactions. Lisa tells them to go find something to do before she finds something for them to do first.

I haven't sat still for this long in years. I have so many questions wandering aimlessly in my brain.

"When am I going home?" I ask.

"I'm not sure, Lainie."

"Okay. When am I going to see my mom next?"

"I'm not sure."

"She'll probably call you from a pay phone because she doesn't have a telephone. And she'll come in a taxi to get us because she doesn't have a car."

"Maybe. I'm not sure what she's going to do."

"I don't want to see Cain, though," I say firmly. "He's still at the motel with her. They were supposed to break up because he's bad to her. I hate him. Mom should have got rid of him instead of us."

"I don't have the answers you're looking for, Lainie."

"Am I going to school?"

"We still have to figure all that out."

Lisa doesn't have the answers to any of my important questions. "Why do you pray to 'Dear God' so much? Who are you really talking to?" I ask. Suddenly she has all the answers. I wish I had never asked. She won't shut up about him.

I interrupt her and ask again, "When am I going to see my mom? I need to get back to the motel before she leaves without us. The taxi always takes us far away. What if she can't call you because she lost your phone number or she doesn't know where you live? How will she know where to find us? She doesn't have any money. Maybe you can give her some for the taxi. They cost a lot."

Lisa sighs. "Lainie, I don't think you'll be living with your mother for a while."

"What do you mean?" I ask. "For how many days?"

"I'm not sure."

"You don't know anything!" I snap in frustration. My chest immediately tightens, and tears form in the corners of my eyes. I'm angry at her for controlling my life. No one seems to care about what I want and need. I feel desperate, helpless, and distraught. My lungs begin to inhale quick, pulsing breaths, and I know I'm on the verge of sobbing and losing control. I jump from the couch and run to my room. I want someone to hold me, but I also want to be alone. I close my door and crawl onto the bottom bunk. I hang my head and stuff my face into my pillow. Pent-up air escapes my lungs, and my muffled cries heat my cotton pillowcase and warm my face. The thought of not seeing my mother or siblings causes physical pain in my chest. I don't know how I'll live another day without them.

"Mom," I whimper to myself. "Why did you let me go?"

CHAPTER NINE

Country Life

SUMMER 1995

I stood in front of the Thompsons' house and tried to imagine it as my new home. The crescent road they lived on was far away from the hustle and bustle of the city life I was used to and felt very private and peaceful. The property anchored several tall, healthy trees to the earth below. The wind blew through their leaves like a song and made me pause and close my eyes. I breathed in the crisp, clean air and released my worries with the exhalation. The fresh and unpolluted air made my lungs feel as if they'd been washed and hung on a laundry line to dry.

I immediately noticed the giant tree growing up through the rust-colored wooden deck of the front porch only a couple feet from the living room window. It was obnoxious but beautiful. I wondered what would happen if it fell on the house with us inside. Across the road was a rich forest springing to life. The forest behind the house was doing the same. Everything was green and alive. The best part was the small, sandy beach only a five-minute walk down their dirt road.

My siblings would love it here.

Lisa points to the neighbor's fence and tells us a man named Bearfang and his wife live there. *Bearfang?* On the streets, people gave each other scary nicknames to represent who they were. I wonder what he did to earn a name like that. I peek between their fence boards and see an in-ground pool and beautiful gardens. Lisa says they like to keep to themselves and warns us to do the same. I decide I am okay with that. Val is the neighbor to the east who lives by himself. Lisa says he is a kind and wonderful man. He doesn't have a fence along his property line, which makes the backyard feel even bigger.

This property and location are a dream come true for a little girl with an abundant imagination. Ellie, my cousins, and I spend endless hours in the forest across the road, catching tadpoles in the swamps. We pretend they're our babies, calling them by name and checking on them daily. When their back legs sprout from their top-heavy bodies, Ellie and I place our hands over our hearts, pout our lips, and say, "Aw, Dapanga and Matilda, you're growing up so fast!" Ellie wants to name her future child Dapanga. I get upset with her about it and beg her not to. I don't want to be an aunt to a Dapanga.

There's a decaying little plywood castle near the back of the property, along Bearfang's fence line; at least that's what I imagine it to be. It's probably an old doghouse that's lost its strength from the many heavy Canadian winters it's endured. At nine years old, I'm tall enough to have my head touch the roof, and when I spread my arms out, I can touch both sides of the walls. Although it looks weak and tired, I imagine it as my strong and mighty fortress. Ellie, my cousins, and I shape an outline of a vehicle in front of it with the fallen branches we find in the yard and near the forest. We lean thin, decaying pieces of wood against broken red bricks for our gas and brake pedals for when we need to go really fast to pass the slowpokes or slam on the brakes to avoid an accident. We're little kids with road rage. We use sturdy sticks as our gear shifters and old, rotting plywood for the backseat. When a sharp turn comes, we grab each other and scream while vigorously swaying to the left and right. We quickly make up the things we need to dodge, such as deer and stray dogs in the middle of the road. We unbuckle our make-believe seatbelts, wipe sweat from our brows from our long, scary journey, and switch drivers.

An enormous, beautiful tree in the backyard dangles its tire swing like a long gold chain with a black-hooped earring. A gentle breeze blows toward the swing and makes it sway softly back and forth, tempting me to wind it up, jump on its back and spin around until I get sick. I can't wait. I could play on it for hours.

We slap the side of the tire repeatedly, making it spin nonstop until the fraying, worn yellow rope twists higher and higher and tighter and tighter. When we can't spin it any further, it's time to jump on. My cousins hold the bottom of the tire still to keep it from swinging. I stretch my left foot up onto the tire's rim and reach to grab the rope with both hands. I use my right leg to kick off the ground and quickly swing it over the tire as if I'm mounting a horse. With a big smile on my face, I look down to my audience, who are all anticipating my dizziness. They let go of the tire, and I lean my head back to begin my unraveling nightmare. I am flying, faster and faster, barely holding on with the tips of my fingers. I use all my might to pull my body closer to the rope to gain some more control, and my long brown hair, which dangles so beautifully down my back, gets caught in the rope. It wraps around the rope repeatedly with every torturous turn, and because I can't stop the tire from spinning, I fear it'll rip the skin right off my head.

I'm sitting like an arrow in a dartboard, rigidly stiff and screaming, begging for someone to run and get Lisa. I feel as though I've been confined forever when I finally see her walking down the steps of the back deck and across the yard toward me. She looks up at me with her hands on her hips and says ever so calmly, "My goodness, Lainie. What did you do to yourself?" She tries to untangle me, but the frayed fibers of the rope have twisted themselves into the strands of my hair. I am too high up and need a ladder for it to unwind without the weight of me on it. It's so painful. Lisa throws her arms out in defeat. "It's impossible to get that untangled, Lainie. I'll be back." And she is, with a stepstool and a pair of kitchen scissors.

My cousins are belly-laughing on the ground. "She's gonna cut your hair off!" one of them says. And she does, right at the scalp. My head looks as if someone has cut a single strip of grass with a lawnmower and run out of gas. I am mortified. I have thick, voluminous, chestnut-brown hair on the sides and a short mohawk down the center. The huge, swollen goose egg I feel pulsing on the top of my head literally looks like the cherry on top. Styling my hair after this tragic accident will be of the utmost importance. There will be no hiding this spiky row of hair once it starts to grow and fan itself out like a peacock. This is devastating. What will my classmates think when I start school? I walk inside the house to the washroom and cry in front of the mirror. As if I need another reason to be made fun of. I desperately try to part my hair to the side, but it falls back into place. I toss my brush, along with the idea of ever being noticed by any of the cute boys at school.

CHAPTER TEN

Living on a Prayer

1995

Lisa has all the children on a daily cleaning schedule that rotates weekly. Each child is responsible for keeping their assigned room or area of the house clean for the entire week, and the following week, they rotate with a sibling. For example, if I clean the living room one week, I clean the bathroom the next, and so on. We each have our own laundry day as well. Lisa inspects our bedrooms daily and expects them to be spotless.

We're on a schedule for meal prep and kitchen cleanup too. We have a dishwasher, but we aren't allowed to use it, because Lisa says she already has six dishwashers (her children) and using it is a waste of water and power. She has task sheets and checklists for everything. For a child like me, who's never had a single rule in her life or ever had to lift a finger around the house, the constant chores and orders make me feel like a servant. However, the rigorous schedules help pass the time and make my life more predictable. It also distracts me from constantly focusing on how much I miss my mom and family.

The television is only turned on by an adult, which rarely happens. Sometimes, as a special treat, we get to watch VeggieTales (a children's Christian cartoon) or, at the odd time, a family movie. We don't have a lot of time for watching screens, with our wild imaginations, our adventures, and all the chores we do. We aren't allowed to use the phone or the computer. We're not to open the fridge unless we've been given permission. We eat at mealtime and that's it. If we don't like something on our plates, we're still expected to eat it, even if it leaves us coughing and gagging in our seats. If we don't eat it, we're required to sit at the table and watch the others enjoy their dessert in front of us while they moan and brag about how good it is.

Lisa makes assortments of mouthwatering fresh breads. I love them all except the raisin bread. I can't stand the texture of warm, wet, slimy raisins in my mouth. Lisa knows I hate it but serves it to me for breakfast anyway. She refuses to make me a unique breakfast. The children around the table watch me gag, on the verge of throwing up, while my red eyes water. I will never like raisin bread, no matter how many times she serves it. It feels like a cruel joke.

Lisa operates like a robot. She is raising me like a soldier and is incredibly hard on me. Still, I am loyal to her and vie for her love and attention. I act and behave my very best to avoid punishment and keep her pleased with me, but it never seems to be enough.

I've developed a severe stutter and still wet my bed often. I outdo all my siblings in chores and then ask for more work to do. *Surely this will make Lisa love me*, I think. I wait for positive praise or physical affection from her, to confirm in my heart that she cares about me, but those words and actions rarely happen. I work hard and do my best to learn everything she teaches me, which is a lot. My only goal is to please her, and I fail daily.

I now know the untreated ear infections I had as a young child made me hard of hearing and affected my speech, and I needed hearing aids. Steve and Lisa tell me repeatedly that I hear only what I want to hear and tell me I have selective hearing. They've never taken me to get my ears checked, and I have difficulty understanding what people say, so I'm always blamed for lying and receive severe consequences I haven't earned.

I am grounded for every nit-picking lie they think I tell, though many times I either didn't understand what they asked or didn't hear what they said. My stuttering worsens when they question me. I'm nervous they'll manipulate my words and punish me with isolation. To them, my stuttering is a dead giveaway that I'm lying, even when I'm not. I'm blamed for things I don't do. Steve can manipulate people into thinking a spoon is a fork, assure them they've committed sins they haven't, or prove they've lied somehow so he can feel superior. I'm afraid to talk to him and even more afraid to be alone with him. I get gross feelings in my belly when I'm around him, and he makes me feel anxious. He talks for hours nonstop about things I don't understand, such as car transmissions and all the intricate parts of an eyeball, then makes me feel clueless for not understanding or remembering what he's said. I've learned to say whatever it is he wants to hear, but then that gets me in trouble too. I'm so stressed and confused whenever he speaks to me. I just stay out of his way and avoid him.

If I lie (and even if I don't but they think I did), I get sent to my room for the entire night with a piece of bread with peanut butter on it and a glass of water. I spend multiple nights every week in my room in isolation. It happens frequently, and the loneliness is tormenting.

Order is always kept within the house. I know where to be and when. There is no talking back, not even to explain myself. If I'm sent to my room, I turn and walk without question. I do what I'm told. Lisa does too. If Steve demands to know which one of the kids did something wrong and no one confesses, we are all sent to our rooms until someone is brave enough to take the blame so we can get out.

One of Lisa's church friends allows her to use a small portion of her family's farm field so our family can grow our own vegetables. Lisa packs all of us kids into her huge van, and we work for hours bent over in the hot sun planting vegetable seeds, pulling weeds, and maintaining the crops. Lisa tells me to pull weeds bent at the waist because lazy people crouch at the knees. When the harvest is ready, we pick an assortment of vegetables and bring them home. The children husk the corn on the back deck and bring it to Lisa to be boiled. We cut the corn off the cob and bag it. We scald the green and yellow beans, cut them up, and bag them too. We stock our freezer full of vegetables for winter and pack our cupboards with various glass jars full of pickled cucumbers, beets, salsas, relishes, and jams made from fresh fruits we picked ourselves from local farms. I love the jams we make. We work hard together and appreciate our food because we grow it ourselves and make it last through the winter months. I am exhausted though. Being bored isn't a possibility here. To survive at the Thompsons', I need to do what they ask, work hard, keep the peace, and do my best to avoid trouble.

I go to church with the Thompsons multiple times a week. It feels like my second home. Lisa is the church's secretary and plays an active role as a "church member." This means she is expected to give tithes and offerings every week and attend special meetings. She also has the privilege of voting on church issues and can also vote on whether a person who has applied for membership is a good fit or not.

On Sundays, our family walks down the aisle of the sanctuary to our seats like ants in a line. We sit in the third row from the front, near the windows on the right side of the sanctuary. If another family sits in our row, we don't know what to do, so we awkwardly stare at them while crowding the area and wait for directions from Lisa. "They're sitting in our spots," we tell her. We aren't allowed to sit anywhere else. Our family makes the situation so awkward that the others leave our church bench. If we get caught chatting with a sibling during service, all Lisa has to do is simply look in our direction, and we immediately sit upright with our hands folded on our lap. If she gives "the look," I worry for the rest of the service what my punishment will be when I get home—either not getting dessert after lunch or spending time alone in my room.

I enjoy learning about the Bible stories Mrs. Hamilton teaches us in Sunday school. Mrs. Hamilton is short and very sweet, and her husband, our lead pastor, looks like a stick bug with glasses. She tells me God loves me unconditionally, which she explains means no matter what, despite all the things I have done wrong. She talks about how Jesus gave up his life to die for me because he loves me so much. I am excited to have someone, even if I can't see him, love me thoroughly, with no conditions, just the way I am. Why does it feel as though love has every precondition at home? Mrs. Hamilton encourages me to pray. She explains to me how God always hears the cries of my heart when I talk to him, and he listens to me too. She talks about this wonderful, all-forgiving, all-loving God who loves me just as I am, but I don't understand. At home, I have to earn his love, and I feel afraid of him. Which one is it?

If it's true that Jesus loves me, I want to do what my teacher and Lisa say, and ask him to live in my heart forever. I sit on the top bunk of my bed and do a repeat-after-me prayer with Lisa, asking God to forgive me for all the sins I have committed and thanking him for dying on the cross. Lisa is proud of me and calls her mom, whom I'm learning to call Grandma, and her best friend, Gina, to tell them the news. I'm not entirely sure what I've done, but Lisa is glowing, and I would do anything to make her proud of me.

* * *

I'm getting baptized today, and Steve and Lisa's son, Caleb, is getting baptized too. I've been looking forward to this day for a few weeks now. I'm going to make God proud, and people too. I'm going to be seen and noticed. People will congratulate me with hugs and affection. Maybe I'll get a baptism gift with a card full of nice words. I'm filled with buoyant energy as I lay out my Sunday dress to wear. Lisa calls me into the kitchen and says I've lied about something. She's angry with me and tells me I'm not ready to be baptized. I'm defensive. I don't understand what I'm being blamed for. I know the consequence for lying is peanut butter on a piece of bread and an entire day of isolation. I wonder whether she'll be cruel enough to do that to me on such a special day. "I'm going to call the pastor and cancel your baptism," she says. I fall to the ground sobbing, losing air and forgetting to breathe. Tears fall from the bridge of my nose onto the floor. I'm absolutely devastated. I look up into her eyes, searching for love and waiting for restoration.

"I try so hard to make you love me!" I cry out, hyperventilating between words. "What will it take to make you love me?"

"Imagine how disappointed God is in you, Lainie." She shakes her head. "He hates liars!"

"Why can't he love me the way I am? I'm a good girl. Why do you think I'm such an awful child? I'll never be good enough for you, and I'll never be good enough for God, either. I try hard to make you and God happy, but no matter what I do, I can't. I hate my life here! I want my family."

If Lisa cancels my baptism, I'll be unseen again in my bedroom. I'm disappointed that I can't live up to their expectations. I can't be perfect. The anger and fear crawling under my skin silences me. I'm not allowed to explain myself anyway. I feel like a complete failure to my family and to God; it's as if I'm constantly on a teetering scale, trying to figure out how much God and Lisa love me.

Lisa grabs the cordless phone and goes to her bedroom to call the pastor as she said she would. I wait in my room, full of fear and anxiety as they discuss the situation. Lisa finally comes out, and I spring up from my bed. "The pastor is willing to baptize you today, but if it was up to me, he wouldn't be." I'm thankful for the grace of the pastor and for the opportunity to tell the congregation about my love for Jesus and his love for me. Deep down, I feel like a hypocrite for trying to convince people I'm good when I've been made to feel the opposite.

I'm elated about the positive encouragement I receive from the church members and feel confident in myself. After the service, I climb into the van to take my place among the siblings. I straighten the skirt of my floral dress before I buckle myself. On the way home, Steve announces he's taking us to Kentucky Fried Chicken to celebrate. We rarely get takeout because it costs so much. This is a huge deal. I'm giddy with excitement. Steve gloats about how good it smells, and I agree. He passes it around to the kids but skips me. "There won't be any for you," he says. "You know the consequences for lying." Ellie turns her head sharply to look at me, then looks back to Steve and furrows her eyebrows. I'm devastated and clench my fists. I hate him and want to tell him how horrible he is, but I know the consequences of talking back or arguing with him. I cry silently in my seat the whole ride home, salivating while my family smacks their lips and licks their fingers. When we get home, Lisa sends me directly to my room. I sit on the bed, fold my hands, and lean forward. Lisa opens the door and places the bread and water on my dresser. I don't even acknowledge her. I grab the plate and sit back down. My wet hair swings forward from behind my back, not even dry yet from being fully immersed in holy water. Tears fall to the laminate floor between my feet. I eat my regular meal and wonder what it means to be a Christian.

The constant loneliness and seclusion from being sent to my room alone hurts me mentally and emotionally.

I remember the days of sitting in my porch box alone, daydreaming and imagining a better life. I realize not much has changed; now I'm alone in a different box, wishing I were outside again with no one looking for me.

The nights I spend without my family are long and lonely. Nightmares invade my sleep. Even breathing feels difficult. It's the loneliest pain I have ever known. At night, I stand by my bedroom window and look up to the moonlit sky, wondering whether somewhere in the world, my family is sharing the same view. It makes me feel closer to them. I crawl into bed and hold tight to Ellie. I know she loves me and wants nothing more than to be close to me. We'll grieve our family together and remember our long-lost days of freedom.

CHAPTER ELEVEN

Loyalty and Visits

1996

My allegiance to Mom is obvious on the weight scale of loyalty. My devotion to her sits like a ton of bricks on one side, and the Thompsons dangle weightless in the air on the other. Days, weeks, and months pass, and I slowly lose sight of the hope of Mom getting us back. I'm used to the predictability and routine of my new life here. The house rules and the expectations of us are concrete. Lisa never changes her mind when she decides on something. I'm desperate for her love and want to call her "Mom." I think it will connect us if she sees me as her daughter. Maybe she'll be more affectionate toward me. I feel conflicted and wonder how I can call Lisa "Mom" without my own mother finding out. I don't want Mom thinking I love Lisa more than I love her. I'm not ready to transfer my life over to the Thompsons just yet. A part of me still hopes I'm only visiting their home, just longer than expected.

One day, we visit with our mother at the old church Steve and Lisa attend. Ellie and I are eager to see her and wonder what we've missed out on since we saw her last. I hear the metal door slam as Mom enters the addition of the church and crosses the original creaky wooden floorboards toward the Sunday school room. The Salvation Army thrift store often gives Mom free toys and stuffed animals for when she visits her children. We're ecstatic to see her carrying two full garbage bags she's dragged onto the city bus and carried all the way here. Ellie and I run and throw our arms around her waist when she approaches us. Mom drops her bags to hug us back. She feels smaller than usual. We haven't seen her in so long, and we beg to know why. She explains that Steve wouldn't allow her to visit us after he gained custody, so she had to take him to court to gain her visiting rights back, and that took a while. The judge granted Mom's visits and ordered Steve to stay fifty feet away from of us during our allotted time together, which he apparently had a hard time obeying. I don't realize how hard it is for Mom to get to our visits on the outskirts of Barrie. I don't even know where she lives. Mom smiles at us from her sturdy plastic chair while Ellie and I play with toys at her feet. Later, she watches me draw bubble letters with colorful crayons, writing "#1 MOM" across my white sheet of paper. Mom loves it and thanks me but tells me I should keep it for myself. Our visits don't last very long, maybe an hour or so. I closely watch the clock on the wall and get anxious as the thin black hand ticks closer to the hour. We lower our voices and talk like secret agents about Mom's plan to get us back.

"I need a house and some money first," Mom says. "I don't have a house or any money right now. I'm broke."

"You can get money from your check," I say. "Where do you live right now?" I'm concerned.

"I'm not allowed to talk about that with you."

"Tell me," I demand.

"The Thompsons don't want you knowing I'm homeless."

She asks what kind of toys we'd like her to bring for us at our next visit and promises to bring them from the thrift store. We ask her where Rosie and Hudson are, and she says they've been taken from her. I'm devastated. She also tells us she's been writing letters to us, but I haven't seen or read any. Why has no one told me any of this news?

Mom's body twitches all the time now. It looks like someone is constantly zapping her whole face and shoulders with a hidden remote control. She talks with her teeth clenched, and her dark lipstick makes it more noticeable that she isn't taking care of her teeth. Her makeup is darker, and she walks as if she's in pain. She wears heavy clothes in the middle of summer and still complains of being cold. She is never super happy or really sad, and I can't remember seeing her cry. Mom's facial expression when she's excited is raised eyebrows, and even that rarely happens. Unless she's getting free food or being given something, her face remains emotionless. I know she's happy to see her children because she smiles when we walk in the room.

Mom's paranoia is nerve-racking and more noticeable than ever. She is easily offended and believes we are laughing at her or saying things behind her back. Ellie and I are having an imaginative conversation with our Barbies when Mom blurts out, "Are you talking about me? Who are you talking about? Did you say I'm ugly?"

We apologize and say no.

"Okay, because those Barbies look like me."

We continue to play and laugh at the silly situations we make up, and Mom blurts out again, "Are you laughing at me? What's so funny?"

"No," we assure her. We talk quieter so she can't hear us. She can't hear very well either.

Mom rotates her pointer finger in circles in front of her when she talks, and she repeats herself constantly. She retells the same story over and over again but is unable to organize her words. She frustrates herself and has to say what she wants without any errors before she can move on to the next subject. I hold her cold, twitching hands and assure her I understand what she's trying to say, even though I don't.

When our visit with Mom is over, we hold her close and cry before Lisa tells us it's time to get into the van. I look out the window toward Mom as she flaps her hand to motion good-bye. Steve takes the bags of toys Mom brought us and throws them on the ground in front of her feet. "I don't know where these came from, and I don't want bugs in my house." *They aren't for you.* He makes me so mad. He could have at least taken them and thrown them away later instead of purposely hurting her feelings like that.

Leaving my mother behind after spending time with her never felt right. She stands in the same spot, waving to us as we drive away in our rusted, poop-colored eleven-passenger van that beeps when it backs up. We wave back until we can't see her anymore. If she can see the van, she stands waving. I don't know where she goes from here. I don't know where she'll sleep tonight. She's alone, and we're supposed to be together.

Once home, I gather the courage to question Lisa about the letters. Lisa says it's true and agrees to read us a couple of them. I love seeing my mother's handwriting, but Lisa tilts the page away from me, and I can tell she's skipping lines. I want to hear everything my mother has to say, not just some. Lisa believes the letters aren't age appropriate for us, and it frustrates me. I want to keep Mom's letters, but she won't allow me to do that either. I love hearing where Mom is, what she's doing, and what my siblings are up to.

CHAPTER TWELVE

School

1995–1998

I am hesitant and hopeful to start fourth grade at a public school in Stroud. I am nine years old and have rarely been to school. Going to school full-time every day will be a lot for me. The days of just running off the school property when I don't want to be there are long gone.

Lisa knows everything and seems to have eyes everywhere. She's our school's bus driver and has a working relationship with the principal.

On school mornings, we watch the clock closely. Lisa, of course, has our schedule planned to the minute:

- 6:00–6:15 a.m.: Wake and clean our bedrooms
  If any items are found on our bedroom floors, we have to pay a quarter per item to Lisa from our two-dollar-a-week allowance. If our beds aren't made tightly and to her liking, we have to pay for that too. By the time she's done deducting quarters, I rarely get any allowance at all.

- 6:15–6:30 a.m.: Breakfast
  We are to be seated at the table and ready to eat by 6:15 a.m. If we appear in the kitchen at 6:16 a.m., we are sent away from the table and go to school without breakfast.

- 6:30–6:45 a.m.: Make lunch
  If we are caught taking more than one slice of bologna or more than two cookies, we don't get any for the rest of the week.

- 6:45–7:00 a.m.: Bible devotions, and prayer for the day

- 7:00–7:15 a.m.: Brush teeth, pack backpack, and get out the door
  Every minute we are late out the door equals five minutes against our bedtimes. If we are five minutes late out the door, we go to bed twenty-five minutes early. Many times, the sun is still shining when I'm sent to bed.

- 7:15–7:25 a.m.: Play outside until Lisa comes outside and starts the bus

Ellie has taught herself gymnastics and passes her time doing acrobatics across the lawn while she waits to board the bus. She can do round-offs, backflips, the splits (both ways), walk on her hands—you name it. I am not that flexible. It is her gift only. When Lisa walks out of the house, we quickly run over to the row of backpacks lined from youngest to oldest in front of the bus's folding doors. We slip them onto our backs and wait for Lisa to enter first.

I sit in the front seat behind Lisa while she drives. I ask her questions and chitchat before we pick up the kids on her bus run in the morning and at the end of the day after we drop them off. I do most of the talking to keep Lisa from telling me all the chores I have to do when I get home. After school, she backs the bus into our long double-wide laneway like a professional. Once the bus is in park, I stand in the aisle and wait for her to open the front doors so we can all race out into the yard.

I remember my first day of school: I eagerly looked around the classroom, smiling at anyone who looked my way, hoping he or she would smile back at me. I anticipated new friendships. I sat up straight at my desk and folded my hands. I envisioned being the top student in my class and getting perfect grades on all my assignments. My teacher placed a picture of a family tree on my desk that included written instructions on how to write a biography about my life. My eyes grew large and teary. Disappointment shrunk my stiff posture into a slouch. My sweaty palms bounced the end of my pencil off my desk, and I immediately began biting the skin of my inner cheek. I lifted my hand in a vigorous panic to ask what I should do. I simply didn't have the answers to this assignment. My teacher saw my struggle and approached me. "Just do your best," she said. I threw the idea of a perfect grade out the window and sat frozen with worry that I'd fail my first piece of schoolwork.

During recess, the students asked questions about where I moved from. I answered every one of them honestly without pause, as though they'd lived similar lives to mine. I quickly learned we were not the same. Most thought my past sounded strange and dangerous, but I thought theirs were boring and lame. I didn't know how to make attachments to other kids. My family moved constantly, and I decided it was better not to attach to other kids, to save myself the disappointment after separation. I feared their rejection. I offered to help my teacher clean the classroom every single recess by wiping down boards, putting away supplies, taking out the recycling, sweeping the floor—anything except going outside to be with the other kids. Sometimes she'd let me stay in and work while I talked her ear off. I didn't want to give her the opportunity to suggest I go outside.

A few months later, Lisa reads my fourth-grade report card from the first term out loud. "'When oral instructions are being taught, Lainie needs to focus her attention on the speaker and concentrate on what is being said.' What is this all about, Lainie?"

I try to explain myself. I wish she knew what it was like for a kid like me to learn. Paying attention is nearly impossible with all the intrusive thoughts invading my mind. I can't remember the teacher's instructions two minutes after she tells them to me. My brain is in a constant state of stress, and I'm distracted by anything and everything. My brain wanders again. I tell her my thoughts feel like a heaping bowl of entangled spaghetti; every thought leads to the slimy path of another, wandering everywhere except for the place it's supposed to be, and I'm lost at the bottom of the bowl, trying to find my way back to where I began. It feels impossible.

Lisa looks at me sideways. "Where do you come up with this stuff, Lainie? Maybe you need to go to bed earlier so you can concentrate better at school. I need to think what to do about this."

Disappointing Lisa is soul crushing to me. She thinks I'm not trying hard enough, but it simply isn't true. I don't want to be in any more trouble at home. I blame myself for my ever-wandering mind and feel foolish for not being able to focus. Maybe I need to stop dreaming. Not only can I not concentrate, but I'm also partly deaf. I take the blame at home and at school for choosing not to listen and again "hearing only what I want to hear." I cup my ears with my hands and pull them forward to help me hear. Most of the time, it helps, but when it doesn't, I ask my peers to repeat the teacher, but they grow easily annoyed by my redundant requests.

Sometimes I have to sit in the back of the class with a specialist who replays various sounds on her tape recorder, pausing each time to ask me what I hear. She will not accept the answers I give, and it frustrates me. The students look to the back of the class, and I instantly feel self-conscious and embarrassed. The specialist repeats herself and plays the sound again. She taps the end of her pen against her notepad repeatedly. "Lainie. Don't pay attention to them. Concentrate on our exercise. Tell me what you just heard." I scream in frustration, on the brink of tears, "For the last time, lady, it's a ——— train!" She quickly packs up her things and tells me we're done for the day. I should have yelled sooner. Why do I need to know what a creaking door sounds like? Or a chip bag being crumpled? What a pointless exercise. I'm ashamed and determined to prevent this situation from happening again. I work harder. I focus my attention on people's lips when they speak to me. I study the movement of their mouths and watch carefully as they pronounce each word. I become so good at lip-reading that I can understand conversations between multiple people, even on the television when it's on mute. Most of the time, I can understand my peers without hearing their voices at all.

I quickly learn to read and fall in love with words, books, and the art of language. In the first year of school, I become a fluent reader with expression and understanding. I make use of the classroom books and borrow them from the library. Whenever the teacher asks for someone to read aloud, I shoot my arm up and wave my hand like a fish swimming upstream. Reading a book feels like plunging deep into a fantastical world full of imagination, adventure, and whimsy. I immerse myself into every story and savor each word. I cling to the edge of every page and feel the emotion of every character. I escape my own reality and don't have to be myself. I delve into stories about friendships and relationships, and envision having both. If I'm reading, I can be anyone, anywhere, instead of being here.

I join the track and field and cross-country teams every year. I place first multiple times and keep every ribbon I win as if it is proof of my worth. Running feels like an escape to freedom. All the lies, distractions, and worries from home and school vanish with every laborious breath.

"You'll never be good enough." *Run, Lainie.*

"You're not trying hard enough." *Run harder.*

"You hear what you want to hear." *Don't stop. Keep moving.*

"She works well below her potential." *They can't catch you.*

"She doesn't complete her work." *Almost there.*

I haven't been late a single day this year and was only absent four times for mandatory appointments. Lisa wouldn't let me miss any days even if I tried.

* * *

On April 21, 1996, near the end of my fourth-grade school year, my almost-seven-year-old little sister, Rosie, who had been living with Lisa's sister, comes to live with us. Ellie and I are thrilled and thank Lisa for reuniting us. It's a joyous day to have another lost family member reunited. We're inseparable. We talk for hours about our childhood and what our lives have been like apart from each other. Rosie tells us about her failed placement at Maggie's house, and Ellie and I tell Rosie about what's been happening at the Thompsons'. Rosie tells us what she went through to be reunited with us and how she cried herself to sleep begging to be with her sisters.

Rosie is adorable. She has tanned skin, dimples, full cheeks, a small button nose, and thick shoulder-length brown hair. Her eyes, like mine and Ellie's, disappear when she smiles or laughs. We spend every moment we can together, talking or playing games of make-believe. We attend each other's weddings several times, reciting our vows, fanning our faces, and yes, even pretending to cry at the altar. We take turns holding each other's flower bouquets and fluffing the trains of our make-believe dresses. Ellie takes on the role of the husband because she has no interest in fluttering about or getting married. She pretends to talk in a deep voice and makes funny faces to her bride while blurting out hilarious things she thinks a husband would say. Our bellies ache from laughing so hard. Her sense of humor has us rolling. She is not the meek, quiet child she once was but is rather outspoken, strong-willed, and true to herself and her feelings.

We aren't allowed to listen to the radio, so we record ourselves singing worship songs on our cassette player. Ellie has nose and ear issues and sounds like she's drowning, but Rosie and I can really carry a tune. Ellie sings the lower notes, so we can't hear her very much, and Rosie and I belt out the higher notes with strength. We hold our chests, close our eyes, and lift our hands to mimic the worship leaders at church. We pretend to be radio hosts and introduce new and upcoming artists by sharing a little bit about them. We listen closely to make sure the host talks us up the way we deserve. After every song, I say, "Well, that was amazing!" before moving on. After many mess-ups regarding lyrics and harmonies, I stop the tape, give a lecture, and say, "Girls, we can do better than this. You're not supposed to be louder than me. I'm the leader of the band and shouldn't hear your voices over mine." The girls roll their eyes, and before they have a chance to argue with me, I quickly count to three and hit the record button. We play the song back and listen to ourselves singing. We're so proud and believe we're ready to tour the world. We discuss names for our new worship band and board our pretend aircraft with other rich, high-class citizens.

Rosie is joining our family camping trip this summer for the first time. Lisa, her four boys, and us three girls, who are together at last, pack up our huge van and make our way to the Collingwood area. Steve stays home most of the time to work, and I feel less anxious without him there. I have a lot of wonderful memories from camp. Lisa runs a tight ship as usual and has chore charts and schedules posted so all of us know where we need to be and when. Church services are twice a day, and attendance is mandatory. Lisa makes her own candy shop full of delicious treats we can earn from doing chores. She prints tickets with dollar amounts on them and "pays" us when our chores are completed. We cash them in for chocolate bars, candy, licorice, gum—all the good stuff. It's such a neat idea; I wish she did it at home too. Some nights, Lisa lets us stay up past our bedtime to play board games with her, like Rack-O, Guess Who, Uno, Dutch Blitz, and more. I never want quality time with her to end.

Mrs. Stella's grade five and six class is studying the Vikings this year. I am enamored by stories of bravery and valor and aspire to those qualities. After weeks of learning about the Vikings, the super-exciting moment comes when the students in our class see the big-boxed television getting rolled into our classroom. Mrs. Stella privately asks to speak to me outside the classroom portable, and I get excited, imagining she'll ask me to hand out the popcorn. Instead, she proceeds to tell me I need to leave class and go sit in the hallway of the school with a book while they watch the movie without me. She tells me Lisa's refused to give me permission to view the movie and that she's terribly sorry. I question Lisa when I get home, and I cry from embarrassment. "The movie is not God-honoring, Lainie. I told your teacher, when the time came to watch the movie, to dismiss you."

"That's how people used to live back then. It's real history."

"What if I gave you a cookie but told you there was just a little poop in it? Would you eat it?"

"What?" I ask, completely confused. "What does that have to do with me watching a movie with my class?"

"You might think it's a good movie to watch with your class, but there's gore and violence, and you don't need to see that." I think of the violence I witnessed when I lived with Mom and the movies I watched with my siblings. Watching *Tales of the Crypt* mentally scarred me for life. "There will be no more discussion or arguments about it."

I don't even have words to argue with her. I'm gobsmacked. It's going to take me days to figure out her analogy. What I do know is that I am utterly humiliated. I might as well have "LOSER" written across my forehead. I can already hear the kids snickering and laughing at me while calling me a Bible thumper. I hate it. I already have a hard time learning, and now I'm expected to know things I'm not allowed to learn about.

I'm failing in the friend area. Ellie is popular at school and a dork at our church youth group. I have friends at church, but hardly any at school. During most recesses, I sit in the bathroom stall or by the edge of the forest, pretending I'm invisible. I can't wait for the year to end.

While the majority of my seventh-grade class is mortified about the idea of public speaking, I'm thrilled. I'm pretending I'm an ostrich and have already memorized my speech. Their eyeballs are bigger than their brains; everyone needs to know about them. My teacher, Mrs. Faye, writes on my report card, "Lainie's speech on ostriches was very original and unique. I was very impressed with her decision to speak as an ostrich. Lainie spoke clearly and with enthusiasm." I'm so proud and laugh with excitement.

My school years should be filled with playful friendships and adventurous fun. It hasn't been that way. I wished for an abundance of self-confidence, inner peace, and security instead of feeling fearful, lonely, overwhelmed, and anxious. My hearing loss and distressing thoughts made learning incredibly difficult. They invaded my mind and prevented me from concentrating. Despite all the learning challenges I faced, and being disadvantaged in comparison to my classmates, I pushed forward and tried my best.

CHAPTER THIRTEEN

It's My Party (And I'll Cry If I Want To)

MAY 15, 1999

The day of my thirteenth birthday is beginning like a dream. Lisa has just asked me if I'd like to skip school for the day to take a trip with her. I have never skipped school or been given permission to be absent while in her custody. I'm in utter shock, and I wholeheartedly agree to have the day off. I don't know where we're going or what we're doing, but I don't even care at this point; I get to spend a rare day of quality time with Lisa, just us. Her asking me to spend the day with her feels like someone has rubbed a genie's lamp for me. I don't have to be a loser at school for a whole day. I am elated and full to the brim with anticipation. My cheeks are hurting from the permanent grin I'm wearing. I beg Lisa the whole way to tell me where we're going, but she won't. After what seems like an eternity, we pull into the Toronto Catholic Children's Aid Society's parking lot. My veins convulse with panic. Lisa explains to me that I'm going to spend the entire afternoon with my youngest brother, Hudson.

Oh, good. You're not leaving me here.

I didn't know seeing Hudson was even a possibility. I haven't seen him since we visited him as a baby. He's almost four years old now. After picking up my brother, Lisa tells me we're going to her parents' house. I feel special and honored to spend the whole day not only with Lisa and my little brother, but also with Grandma and Grandpa, whom I see only on special occasions throughout the year. This is the best day I can think of, and I can't wait to get home and tell my sisters.

I'm deep in thought as usual, daydreaming with my head lost in the clouds. I'm thinking about how jealous my siblings are that I got to miss school today. I imagine Mrs. Stella calling out my name during attendance while looking through her oversize spectacles toward my empty seat, and then gasping in shock to see I'm not there. I imagine telling my sisters I saw our baby brother, who is no longer a baby. I imagine Lisa's love for me rising like the red fluid in a thermometer on a hot day, rising from below freezing all the way to the burning top. Mostly, selfishly, I'm dreaming about my birthday party tonight.

At the Thompsons', the birthday child gets to choose his or her favorite meal to eat. For me, it's tacos every single year. Lisa normally makes our cake from a box and smothers it in fluffy whipped icing with our names written across the top. Sometimes she cuts the cake in half and adds a can of cherry filling to make it fancy. We can even choose to have a friend over and get a couple of presents, too. Today isn't just any birthday; it's extra special for a huge reason: I am officially a teenager!

I've invited my older brother Dylan to come to my birthday as my special guest. He's coming from his foster home in Barrie, and I can't wait to see him. Lisa is allowing us to have s'mores and roast hot dogs over the campfire just beyond the tire swing after dinner. To make my birthday feel even more extraordinary, Lisa has made a "practice" three-tiered wedding cake for someone who is getting married from our church, and I will have the honor of eating it for dessert.

I excitedly say hello to Grandma and Grandpa when we arrive at their house and remind them that it's my birthday, just in case they forgot. Lisa asks me to play outside with Hudson in the backyard while she visits with her mom and dad inside the house. I follow Hudson to the cement pad off the porch as he races toward a little red wagon close to the house and climbs into it. I pull him around in large circles, looking straight ahead, singing a song, and anticipating the evening. I hear Hudson cry out in pain. In my daydreaming excitement, I didn't realize he had stood up in the wagon and fallen out and bumped his head. I run in to tell Lisa that Hudson's forehead is red and has a cut on it. She looks at his face and then furrows her eyebrows at me. I lower my face and close my eyes. I feel horrible. I know by the tone of her voice that I'm going to suffer a terrible consequence.

"What happened, Lainie? Tell me, now!"

I panic. "I don't know," I lie.

"You know what happens when you lie," she says sternly. "Go wait in the car."

My visit with my little brother is cut short. He's going back to the children's aid building early, and I'm in big trouble. Lisa packs up Hudson and sees me in the backseat of the car. "How am I supposed to bring him back with a bump on his head? We only had him for a few hours, Lainie!" I decided to sit in the backseat beside Hudson because I'm too ashamed to sit in the front with Lisa. She's silent for a while during the drive to the society, then she speaks up and demands I tell her the truth. So I do, and she hands out the punishment. Instead of having tacos for my birthday dinner, I'll be given a slice of bread with peanut butter, a glass of water, and be sent to my room for the entire night.

I reach for Hudson's thin, smooth hand and rest my head against his car seat. I love him and don't want him to go back to the agency; I want him to come home with us. I worry I'll never see him again, because most good-byes in my life have been final. When we arrive at the agency, Lisa tells me to wait in the car while she brings Hudson inside. I want to bring him in too, but I don't argue with her. I rest my forehead on the cool car window and wave a sad good-bye to my brother as he walks away from me. My thoughts feel torturous, and I'm swallowed by guilt. I want to stand outside to feel the breeze because it's hot in here, but I don't dare leave the car.

When Lisa finally exits the building and makes her way back to the car, she asks whether I want to sit in the front seat with her for the long ride home. I decline. I know she's disappointed in me, and it makes me feel awful. All I want is to make her proud and to have her love me unconditionally. My birthday joy blows through the open air and into the streets when she starts the car and rolls the windows down. My heart fills with pain and disappointment. I reminisce about the traumatizing memories of sitting in this very seat, being taken from my mom and family four years prior. Being in this seat without my baby brother makes me feel as if it's happening all over again.

When we pull into the laneway of our house, Lisa tells me to go directly to my room. I walk through the doors and see my sisters. They wrap their arms around me and shout, "Happy Birthday!" I hold them tight while sobbing, then release them and go to my room as I've been told. They ask Lisa why I'm crying, and she tells them to mind their business. Betrayal, abandonment, and worthlessness sting my heart repeatedly, and I am reminded of how poorly I've been loved my entire life. I regret the invisible life I live in this lonely room. I'm not expecting my birthday party to carry on without me, but it does. I press my warm cheeks down on the cold floor and close one eye to peek through the small crack beneath my bedroom door. I'm hoping my sisters walk in my direction, but Ellie and Rosie have been told not to come into our room, even if they need something. I try to hear what they're talking about, but I can't. I cup my ear, which helps me to hear better, but it means I can't see anything beneath the door. I want to feel a part of their conversation too. I gasp and hold my breath when I hear Dylan's voice. *He came. He's here.* He's brought a gift I will cherish for years—a Winnie the Pooh backpack with leather straps I will see tomorrow.

The Thompsons have to change their mind. They can't be this cruel, can they?

Yes, they can.

The clanging of plates and the familiar savory aromas of taco spices lets me know they're enjoying my favorite birthday dinner without me. Steve rudely mocks me by leading the family in singing a depressing version of happy birthday to me as loudly as they can, making sure I hear them. After dinner, they blow out my flaming dreams with their hateful breath and eat my special three-tiered birthday cake. At sunset, they have the bonfire I asked for in the backyard and roast marshmallows and hot dogs.

I slide open my little bedroom window and smell the campfire air flowing by. I listen to the sounds of my family's laughter and begin to sob uncontrollably. I feel like a prisoner. I imagine the cold window kissing my flushed forehead as I lean against it for support. I raise my wet, glossy eyes to the moon and wonder where Mom and Rachel are. My broken heart is shattered beyond repair. Tonight solidifies many things for me. One, I still don't belong at the Thompsons'; and two, they for sure don't love me.

A year later, Steve and Lisa are finalizing the adoption for Hudson. We've run out of room in our tiny house for any more people to live here. Our little home goes up for sale, and we begin our move to a small town outside of London, Ontario. I'll miss the countryside, but I'm excited to move. I think about Mom and all the places we've been together. I've learned over the years not to get attached to people, so I'm not heartbroken over leaving anyone. I promise to write to a few people but know I won't.

I'm okay to start over somewhere new. For me, life is like an Etch A Sketch board. I hold tightly to its frame with both hands and gaze upon the life that will soon become memories. Then I shake it up and down to erase the past and begin to draw again.

CHAPTER FOURTEEN

Get Me Out of Here

2000–2003

The new house feels massive in comparison to our country home. There isn't a beach close by or forests in the front and back of the house, but it's in a subdivision and less isolated. I miss our big yard already, but I'm excited to be surrounded by new people close by.

I can see our new school from our front yard. It's just past the stop sign at the end of our road. No more riding the school bus to and from school. I start eighth grade in September. I feel disadvantaged starting my graduating year of elementary school with girls who have spent their whole lives growing up together. The girls in my grade are wonderful and do their best to include me in their lives outside of school, but of course, I am not allowed. Every time they invite me out, I beg Lisa, but her answer is always no. I want to be at slumber parties with my friends. I want to leave the school property and go to their houses for lunch, but Lisa refuses to write the permission note I need to let me go with them. I sit alone during lunch and eat my every-day bologna sandwich, then go outside for recess and wait by the fence for the girls to return.

I'm excited to graduate elementary school. Lisa bought me a thrifted blue dress with white polka dots and thick shoulder straps. Every other girl's dress is poofy with shimmering colors and skinny shoulder straps. I lie and tell my friends how expensive my dress was, but they don't believe me. I'm not allowed to attend the dance reception after graduation with my friends and classmates because dancing, especially to worldly music and with other boys around, is sinful. I feel constantly embarrassed by our lifestyle and want to feel like a normal teenager and have freedom outside the church.

Grade nine is the same. Church. Chores. School. My craving for acceptance, relationships, love, and independence has me bursting at the seams. I'm constantly in trouble and now being grounded from youth group and church events. In grade ten, I'd had enough.

One night, when Lisa is at church, Steve comes out of his bedroom in his underwear and housecoat and announces we are going to play a game of hide-and-go-seek. He wants to play the game with ice cubes. Steve turns out all the lights and yells, "Go!" and the kids scatter. He immediately chases me into the bathroom, locks the door behind himself and molests me. The kids bang on the door, and finally, after what feels like forever, he runs out of the bathroom to the other kids, as though nothing has happened, leaving the melting ice cube in my underwear, and me, in tears. Lisa is the closest person I have to a mother. When I tell her what Steve did to me, she refuses to believe me and defends her husband, saying he would never do that. I disconnect from her instantly. I no longer trust her and avoid Steve like it's my job. I feel disgusted by them and don't want to live in their house anymore.

My mother is visiting us at the Thompsons' today. I am excited to see her after so much time apart. During the visit, Steve tells Hudson his Aunt Annie is here to see him.

Mom pats her lap and holds out her hands, "Come see Mommy, sweetie. It's okay,"

"No. You're not my mommy," Hudson says nervously, backing away from her.

Mom starts twitching. Her own son doesn't recognize her. Mom's heart is crushed, and I'm furious about what I'm witnessing. They're erasing my mother from my brother's life and giving her the status of aunt. How dare they do that. Why can't he call his own mother his mom? I look to my twitching mother and back to Steve.

I can feel my body swelling with anger and annoyance. My jaw clenches and my fists follow suit. I stand tall and breathe in to puff out my chest. With all the courage I can muster, I bravely respond,

"She's his mom, *not* his aunt!" I flick out my arm, pointing toward Lisa. "That's his aunt." I point back to my mother. "That's his mom!"

I can't believe it. I can't believe I just said that. Oh, this feels powerful. I feel tenacious and brave. I've been storing that pent-up frustration toward him for years. I want to punch him right between the eyes the way my brother hit Cain.

Steve sticks his pointer finger out at me. "You're not going to say anything else."

"Why, because you're embarrassed of my mom?" Steve's eyes grow large, and he comes closer to stand over me. "She's his mom, and you can't change that. If you don't tell him, I will. He has the right to know." I surprise myself by speaking up again.

I know from the look on Steve's raging face that I'll be in huge trouble. He immediately demands that I go to my room and marches behind me like a cloud of fury with thunder in his footsteps. With his one hand on my doorknob, he threatens, "If you say anything to Hudson, you won't be living here anymore. That's a promise. Test me; I dare you. You'll be outta here so fast."

I tell him again that Hudson has the right to know who his mother is.

"Shut your mouth!" He screams, startling me. "You'll be in your room all day today for your behavior. You won't be seeing your mother." He smiles before he slams my door.

"What else is new?" I mumble to myself.

I hated the pain I saw in my mother's eyes. I hated the confusion I saw on Hudson's face. I am brimming with anger. How dare they keep me from Mom after not seeing her for so long. Steve and Lisa didn't ask how any of this would make me feel prior to my mother coming over, nor did they discuss my feelings afterward. There's been no explanation given to Hudson about who his mom actually is.

I am a fifteen-year-old girl being threatened with removal from the house for telling my brother about his mom. I take Steve's threat seriously. I refuse to be abandoned again, so I decide to make an escape plan before he kicks me out. I don't know where I'll end up, but I have safe adults in my life from church who are aware of the manipulation and control happening inside our home and are willing to help me find somewhere to go. Thanks to Lisa, I know how to cook, clean, budget, and work hard. I know I can take care of myself.

I am sure I can do this. I'm determined to change my life. I will not be kept from my mother and older siblings. Steve will never treat my blood like that in my presence ever again. I will not be used as a pawn in the Thompsons' manipulative, calculated, dark, deceptive lives. Their unending punishments will stop, because I refuse to be a prisoner from this moment forward. I will never eat another peanut butter sandwich again or be punished for things I did not do. I will not keep quiet about what goes on in their home or keep Steve's and his sons' perverted secrets. Lastly, Steve and Lisa will never have the opportunity to threaten me with being unhoused again. I will prepare myself mentally to follow through with my promises.

I tell my youth leaders, Logan and Maria, what's happening at the house, and they immediately intervene. They live with Logan's mom and dad, Greta and Evan Porter, who are straight-up, honest people. There are no gray areas in Greta's mentality. She calls truth what it is and is as confident as they come. She stands up against abuse and injustice and is never afraid to speak her mind. She is a tall, thick, motorcycle-riding woman—exactly the kind of person I need in my life. She protects me, and I feel safe with her. She's been praying for me for years, and I've been on her heart lately. She and her husband know I need to get out and are willing to help me. I'm thrilled when they welcome me to come and live with them. We make plans for me to leave the coming Sunday morning.

The church service begins at 10:30 a.m. and starts with a half hour of worship. I ask my friend Sarah to drive from her house to mine at 11:00 a.m. sharp and to be ready for me to jump into her getaway car. I'm supposed to be helping with the children's ministry this morning. My plan is to wait until the congregation finishes singing and the preacher dismisses the kids to their Sunday school classes, then get up from the pew, usher the kids out of the auditorium to their classes, and discreetly walk out the side door and race home. I have walked from our house to the church hundreds of times before and know it's only an eight-minute speed-walk away. I run as fast as my legs will go to give myself enough time to get into the house, throw my stuff together, and leave before the family catches me or finds out.

Sarah is right on time and waiting for me in the laneway. I grab a few belongings and run out of the house. I open the car door, throw my bag in, and tell her to burn rubber. Greta, Evan, Logan, and Maria meet at the Thompsons' house after the service to explain my absence. I am shaking in my boots as I wait for the Porters to call Sarah's cell. *This has to work out. It just has to.*

Greta tells me later that Steve talked in circles for hours, trying to manipulate her, but she wouldn't have it. Greta saw past his mind tricks. He belittled her by saying, "Let me talk in terms that maybe even you would understand ..."

The Porters offer the Thompsons several solutions, but Steve and Lisa decline them all. Greta and Evan offer to take me during the week and have me go back on weekends; Steve and Lisa decline. The Porters offer to set up free counseling for me; Steve and Lisa decline. The Porters offer to take me for three months, and once again, Steve and Lisa decline saying, "If Lainie leaves now, she's never welcome back here again." That was fine with me. I never wanted to go back. Finally, the Porters leave the Thompsons' house and call Sarah's cell phone. "It's over, Lainie. You'll be staying with us for however long you need."

I cry. I shake. I release all my fears and laugh. I hug my friend too hard. Just to be alone in a car with her feels so freeing. I feel invincible, as if I could fly to the moon with the fuel of excitement rattling in my bones. I roll down the car's window and scream out loud, "I'm free!" I don't care about anyone's glare from the sidewalk. The Porters have unlocked my cage and released me. I'm determined to learn how to fly with broken wings. It may take longer to get where I'm going, but I'll make it there eventually. I am allowed to be me, and I'm excited about it. *But your sisters and Hudson ...* I'll worry about them later.

I don't even think to call the agency after I leave, because I haven't seen their workers in years. I'm not sure whether Steve and

Lisa call them to make them aware, but no one contacts me or checks in at all. I feel forgotten. For years I had told everyone I was adopted to gain a sense of belonging, but Steve and Lisa never did adopt me. They had legal custody of me, Ellie, and Rosie, and only adopted Hudson. I think about that. I feel illegitimate and as if I don't belong, even more so than I already did.

Regardless of the information, I'm no longer willing to live in a household of manipulation, fear, and control, and I'm happy I did what I did. I thoroughly love Lisa, and I'm sad our relationship has come to an end. I'm shrinking in guilt knowing that my three other siblings still live there.

CHAPTER FIFTEEN

The Porters

I'm in awe when I approach the Porters' huge Victorian house. It's stunning. The atmosphere in their home feels fun, safe, and peaceful. The family jokes with me, encourages me, and listens to me when I share my heart. They aren't afraid to show affection or offer an embrace when I'm falling apart or struggling to process the last seven years, or the eight years prior to that with my mother. Greta isn't one to butter me up or say things just to make me feel better. She calls a spade a spade and isn't afraid to speak the truth, even if it hurts my feelings. I try hard to be likable and positive, but I need to grieve, and Greta knows it. She calls out my fears and speaks against them in the name of Jesus. She replaces lies with the truth like a sword through an enemy. I feel safe with her and trust her to lead me.

Greta sees I'm timid and nervous at the dinner table. "Go ahead, Lainie. Fill your plate," she says. Lisa always lined our plates up on the counter and portioned our meals prior to eating. I do as she says and portion my plate without taking too much. I don't want anyone mad at me. I want to make sure there's enough for everyone. There is plenty left over. I want more but don't dare ask.

"Would you like seconds? You can help yourself, Lainie. I don't need to serve you."

"I'm allowed to have more?" I ask, swinging my feet nervously under the table.

"Of course. There's plenty of food to go around here."

I eat until I can't anymore. After supper, Greta brings me upstairs and shows me the room I'll be staying in.

"There's no lock on the door," I say, pointing to its handle.

"We could put one on for you if you'd like."

"No, it's just weird." I pause. "It doesn't lock from the outside."

"Why would we lock it from the outside, Lainie?"

"To keep me in," I say.

"Oh, Honey, we don't do that around here."

My mind feels as if it's running at full speed on a treadmill. I've lived in fear for many years and constantly feel scared and nervous. I can't even muster up the courage to say excuse me to someone standing in my way, because I'm petrified people will think I'm rude or, worse, be disappointed in me, so I just stand there and wait until they move. I've developed learned helplessness, just like Mom. I don't speak up for myself or take chances. I live as though I have been drained of all confidence and do only what I've been given permission to do. I please and perfect. That's the role I've assigned myself to.

While I love the new changes in my life, my heart still aches for my three younger siblings. Ellie and Rosie email me from school, and their letters break my heart. Lisa has removed my photo from the lineup of family members on the wall and has directed the girls not to talk to me because she believes I'm a bad influence now that I've moved out.

I love living with the Porters. I'm the youngest in a house full of adults. There aren't any screaming, arguing children running around. There isn't anyone telling me I need to babysit tonight or rattling off a list of chores that need to be completed. No one is rushing me out the door to volunteer at church. There isn't a constant background noise of authority. It's quiet here. No one is mad or disappointed in me. It's a strange feeling. I get to be a fifteen-year-old girl who is learning to care for myself. I get to breathe and think about me for once. I can lie in the stillness of an early morning and enjoy an entire room to myself. I have no one fighting over my clothes. I can have a bubble bath instead of a timed shower. I can freely sit at the antique desk beside my bed and write poetry or journal about how I'm feeling. I can concentrate on my studies and complete my homework. Huge burdens have been lifted from my shoulders. I can breathe here. I can experience peace.

Shortly after I move in, I start my first job as a cashier at a grocery store in town. I'm thrilled about making my own money. Working as a cashier is much better than the paper route Ellie and I had. We hated that low-paying job. We were embarrassed by it. If we saw people we knew on our route, we'd hide in the bushes or wait on a person's porch with our backs to the road, so they didn't recognize us. I'm not embarrassed to be a cashier. I feel independent and mature to be paid by the hour. I'm incredibly pleasant and bubbly to every customer who enters the store—until he or she places a dozen bags of uncoded produce I've never seen before on the belt. It feels like a bad teacher has just surprised me with a stack of pop quiz papers. I try to hide the small sting of panic on my face, trying not to sound clueless.

"And what is this item called?" I ask for every unrecognizable plant, fruit, and vegetable. I feel like an imbecile. I have no idea what a mango is, or a dragon fruit, or a papaya, or even a kiwi. And then there is all the greenery they're buying. *You've got to be joking.* If it isn't romaine or head lettuce, I don't have a clue what it is. We ate plain food with my mom and the Thompsons. I was wasting their time and getting frustrated with their diets. *How am I supposed to memorize the bajillion number combinations for everything here? And who needs this much produce? Start your own garden, stay home, or pick another lane.*

Evening motorcycle rides with the Porters are my favorite. Greta and Evan both have their own motorcycles, and Logan and Maria ride together on theirs. We embrace the beauty of the evening sky, riding without hurry or destination. Greta's mini-Doberman pinscher sits harnessed in his furry cushioned seat behind the windshield. He smiles during the entire ride as his ears flop in the wind. Behind his goggles, he's on the lookout for Tim Horton's, a Canadian coffee shop, hoping for a plain Timbit and the last sip of Greta's coffee. I feel peace in my heart and gratefulness toward Greta and Evan for all they've done for me. I embrace the falling sunset and the breeze through my hair as we ride into the cool of night, toward home.

After a year of living with Greta and Evan, I work up the

courage to tell Greta I want to live with my big sister, Rachel. I know this hurts her deeply, but I need my biological family. I ask Greta whether it's okay, and she responds, "I will not give you permission, Lainie. It will be your choice." I make my decision, knowing I've hurt Greta's heart, and call Rachel and her husband, Shawn, to come pick me up with my niece, their two-year-old daughter.

I settle into my new life in St. Thomas and soak in my missed time with Rachel. I enjoy spending my days with my big sister. We blast Shania Twain through the house and dance and sing together. We spend our evenings cooking, going for walks, and watching episodes of *Friends* on TV. She teaches me, encourages me, and includes me in her family. Rachel, Shawn, and their bouncy blue-eyed, blonde-haired daughter, Kyra, live in a small two-bedroom house in a quiet part of town near a giant statue of an elephant named Jumbo. I share a room with Kyra, and I love it. We have such a special bond with each other. She lights up my mornings when she peeks through her crib rails and smiles at me, and again before she closes her eyes at night.

Rachel is a dreaming, goal-driven, entrepreneur. She's high on life and full of motivation. She's also brilliant, resourceful, and street-smart. She holds the intricate memories of my childhood—the unique parts of me that make me who I am. I crave hearing stories about our lives and how she took care of me. She tells stories of us in such a visual way, and I listen to them like a child at her feet. She can revisit the past and make me feel as though I'm right there with her.

She's registered me for high school, where I will start my eleventh grade in September. I'm eager to meet new people and focus on my studies. The school year starts so well. I've joined the cross-country team, the track and field team, and the school musical called *SUDS*.

Then winter hits.

CHAPTER SIXTEEN

Finding Mom

On Christmas Eve, 2002, Mom calls Rachel from a city street pay phone. I notice the worried look on my sister's face.

"Who is it?" I mouth to Rachel.

"Mom," she whispers, covering the speaker. "She sounds really sick."

"Where are you, Mom?" Rachel asks. After a brief pause, Rachel responds, "Okay, we'll be right there." Rachel hangs up the phone, grabs her purse, and tells me to get into the van. I waste no time and do what she says.

"Mom lives in St. Thomas?" I ask, bewildered.

"Yes," Rachel answers as she fumbles with her keys. "There's a lot you probably don't know."

We both recognize Mom's blonde wig and her dark makeup right away. Tears form in the corners of my eyes, and I cover my mouth with my coat's sleeve. I haven't seen Mom in so long. I recognize her bleached hair and slouched posture. She's nearly frozen, pulling a black radio behind her back by its cord with one hand and gripping tightly to a large black garbage bag with the other. She's been dragging both behind her back through the cold, wet snow night after night. Mom's children were placed in various homes in 1995, which means she's been unhoused for over seven years. Seeing Mom so weak and tired stretches my heart. I know I'll retain the memory of this day for the rest of my life.

I jump out of the car and hug Mom. "Hi, Lainie." She hears my sniffled cry and repetitively pats my back. "I know. I'm okay."

Rachel helps Mom into her van and drives her to the hospital and registers her at the nurse's station. The nurse hands Mom a small plastic cylindrical cup with an orange lid and a clear medium-sized Ziploc bag.

"We'll need a urine sample from you, Annie. The washroom is located down the hall to the right. Make sure the lid is closed tightly on your cup. Then put it in the bag, zip it closed, and bring it back to me when you're finished, okay?"

The nurse slides her window closed and expects Mom to go find the washroom. Mom is staring through the glass at her, giving her a dirty look.

"So rude, closing the window on me like that," Mom says, annoyed.

"Come on, Mom," Rachel urges. "The washroom is over here."

Mom is suspicious of the woman behind the glass window.

"Why did she close the window on me like that? She doesn't want to talk to me? What is this for, anyway? Why do I have to pee in this? I have the right to know."

We tell Mom again it's so they can make sure her kidneys are okay because she's urinating blood. After some coercion, Mom complies and fills her urine sample cup. I can't believe what I see. Her urine is a dark red and brown color. *Gross.* I ask Mom where the sample bag is, and she goes back into the bathroom and puts her urine cup into it. The nurse slides the window open, takes Mom's sample, places it on the shelf behind her, and closes the window again. Mom glares an untrusting stare toward the nurse, who is becoming visibly uncomfortable. Mom bangs on the glass window and points toward her urine cup. She doesn't trust this process at all and is becoming increasingly paranoid.

"Why did you put that on the shelf?" Mom asks, twitching. "What are you going to do with that? Who are you giving that to? Are you going to leave that there? Someone needs to take that. You better tell me."

Both Rachel and the nurse try to reassure Mom it's for the doctors to make sure her kidneys are okay, but Mom doesn't believe either of them. She bangs on the window again.

"Mom, calm down. It's okay. It's supposed to be there." Rachel explains. "The doctors are just going to look at it and see what's wrong."

"Open this window! What are you doing with that cup? Are you trying to kill me? Are you tricking me? Give it back to me! Get it off the shelf! Why aren't you answering me?"

The nurse picks up the phone and calls the police who are outside the emergency room doors. Mom panics and bolts through the hospital's automatic doors, past the officers, and down the street, screaming, "They're trying to kill me!" After a quick conversation with the nurse inside, the police officers get in their cruiser and chase after my mentally ill mother down the road. They put her screaming, struggling body into the backseat of their vehicle and bring her to the psychiatric ward.

Rachel's completely baffled. "What the heck just happened?"

"I wasn't expecting that either." We're both in awe.

"Honestly, that *really* just happened, Lainie?" She's shaking her head, trying to convince herself. "Oh, my God. Did you see her urine sample? It's all blood. She could die, Lainie."

The thought of Mom dying feels excruciating. Through tears, I ask, "What do we do now?"

"I don't know," she says. "I'll make some calls."

We grab a late-night coffee and head home to anxiously await the hospital's call. Time lingers under the glow of the lamplit living room. We sip our coffees and watch the colors from the muted television show ricochet off the Christmas tree's dangling silver tinsel. When the phone finally rings, Rachel puts it on speaker. "Hi, Rachel. It's Dr. Malone. I've had time to see your mother and assess her situation. I just want you to know you could have very well saved your mother's life tonight." My eyes widen. I lay my head in Rachel's lap to be comforted. She combs her fingers through my hair as the doctor continues. "Annie is lucky to be alive. I'm not sure how much longer she would have survived without antibiotics. Your mother is very sick."

After a short stay in the psych ward, Mom recovers and is released from the hospital with nowhere to live. Rachel registers Mom for government funding to help with the cost of rent and food for the month, then searches newspaper ads and online rentals to find Mom an apartment she can afford in our city. The apartment isn't the nicest place, but the rent is cheap, and Mom won't be too far away from where we live. Mom doesn't have the ability to take care of herself or her living space, but we clean it up as best we can and set Mom up with new dishes and furniture and other things she needs from the thrift store.

* * *

It's been a couple weeks since Mom moved in, and the winter temperatures aren't letting up. It's so frigid my nostril hairs grow frost on them with every sniffled inhale. Rachel and I are heading out to run a few errands. We crank the heat in the van and drive downtown.

"Is that Mom?" I shriek to Rachel. She's in her normal slouched position, walking with her head down to block her face from the whipping snow. Her gait makes it look as if her hips are hurting. Her nose is red. Her bare hands must be freezing.

"Looks like she bought herself a new radio." I say, watching Mom pull it by its cord.

We both can't help but laugh.

"What does she drag around in that bag, anyway?" I ask.

"That whole garbage bag is filled with makeup and mirrors."

"Why, though? I don't understand."

"She's a vain woman. Her looks are very important to her."

"She's got pounds of makeup on her face and wears the same dirty clothes every day."

"You know, Lainie, I hate seeing her like this too, but she's lived this way for as long as I can remember, and you know what? It doesn't bother her. It's other people who have the problem with it."

I think about that and feel guilty about my judgment toward Mom.

Rachel finds a place to park up the street, and we wait for Mom to approach the van. As Mom walks up, Rachel rolls the window down. Gusts of freezing wind consume the warmth of the van.

"Mom!" Rachel yells to the wind. "Mom!" She yells again. Mom's hearing is getting worse, and the sound of the wind and traffic doesn't help. I shout from the passenger side, "Mom!" She finally turns around.

"Oh. Hi, Rachel. Hi, Lainie. I'm just heading to the thrift store. I'm going to bring this radio back. It doesn't work."

No kidding.

"Do you need a ride there?" Rachel asks.

"No, it's not too far away. Thank you, though."

"Are you okay? Do you need anything?"

"You can give me some money if you want."

Mom's love language is receiving gifts, especially money. We gather the change in the car and hand it to her. It isn't much, but it's what we have.

"You look like Jack Frost, Mom," I add. Where are your gloves? You're going to freeze to death out here."

"They got wet and stinky, so I threw them away."

"Okay, look for some at the thrift store while you're there." I suggest.

"Okay. I might not have enough money for that though." Mom looks to the van's cupholder to see if we missed any coins. "Okay then, I love you both."

"We love you too, Mom. Try to stay warm."

"Okay, I love you," she repeats.

"We love you too, Mom," we say again.

I always thought the way Mom waved good-bye was cute. Rather than waving her hand from side to side, she shook her whole hand up and down as though she was tapping a dog on the head.

"Bye, Mom."

I roll my window up and watch Mom continue up the frozen sidewalk.

"I don't know what else to do for her, Lainie. This is the only life she knows."

"It's heartbreaking." I feel a lump forming in my throat. "If I had all the money in the world, she'd have everything she needed."

Rachel and I continue our errands and go about our day. Our

bond is unshakeable. She's my favorite cook, the best finger-pointing-in-the-sky dancer, and an A-for-effort singer. She is my best friend. We run together for exercise, then go and get ice cream. We take long walks around town, then get chips and queso. We take up inline skating which is a lot of fun. Rachel gives it up after she crashes into our neighbor's bushes while they are relaxing on their porch. Her body and ego are so bruised that we both stop skating right away.

Rachel is very protective of me but knows I need to grow in my independence. I need a job and a way to provide for myself. Rachel helps me create a résumé, and we deliver them around town. I get a job at a convenience store called the Westside Dairy Hut, close to home. I'm seventeen years old, still in eleventh grade full-time, and working until eleven in the evening. Things are going great until I grow big eyes for Nick, my boss's twenty-one-year-old son. He's six feet tall, incredibly charming, and as confident as they come. I think I've fallen in love with him, but I don't know what safe love is yet. Rachel has bad feelings about him and tells me it isn't safe. When she tells me not to date him, I pack my things and move in with my friend Amber, who lives in a beautiful farmhouse outside of town and raises horses for pleasure.

I should have listened to Rachel, and Amber too.

After only two months of dating, Nick enters the store holding an eight-week-old boxer puppy in his arms and asks me to move into his home. I'm happy to take care of him and excited to feel like a woman. During the next six months, my siblings find out about his drug use and him abusing me. I become hospitalized from Nick's abuse and am blamed for cheating with the doctor after being examined by him. Nick has isolated me from everyone I love and has full control of me. I'm not to tell anyone what happened, especially Rachel.

I allow Nick to crush what's left of my self-worth. His voice rings loudly in my ears, "You will never amount to anything, Lainie! You hear me? You will never be more than the ——— on my shoes! You'll be passed around, just like your mother. *No one* will *ever* love you!"

His words cut deep and settle under my skin like a bad tattoo.

When I find Nick cheating on me, I lose control of my mind and body and throw a raging fit. I'm barely over a hundred pounds, but I kick and punch him, and cry and scream. Nick calls the police, then hangs up, and mockingly sings that I'm going to jail. The police arrive and put me into the backseat of their cruiser and take me to the county jail. Before taking me out of their car, the officers turn and offer their support saying they removed me from Nick's house in hopes that I don't go back. This isn't the first time they've responded to a call about him.

After being fingerprinted and photographed from all sides, I'm left crying and shaking in a cold jail cell, alone.

I'm not a criminal. How did I get here?

A few hours later, I'm allowed to call Rachel, who picks me up and comforts me. The next day, she helps me apply for a restraining order and counters Nick's charges against me. I have mountains of evidence against him, and he's in school to become a police officer. Days before the trial, Nick drops his charges and is never to be seen again.

CHAPTER SEVENTEEN

Finding My Way

2004–2006

I find a room for rent in St. Thomas with a single woman named Barbara. She has no children of her own and has worked in the police force for over twenty years. She's always wanted to mentor youth and is a perfect mix of fun and sensibility. Her house is immaculate, and everything in it is expensive and perfectly placed. Her backyard looks as if it were cut out of a magazine, and her boxer lying in the yard reminds me of my last puppy. Her house feels like a home.

Barbara lifts my spirits and keeps me distracted. We go on day trips together. We dress up in over-the-top Halloween costumes and take part in every magical thing there is to do and see during the Christmas season. On my eighteenth birthday, Barbara brings me to see Chippendale dancers at a club to celebrate me being an adult. I'll never forget what I see and experience for as long as I live. We cook together, try new restaurants, watch romantic comedies in her massive bed, and usually fall asleep before the movies end. We have too much wine, turn into prunes in her hot tub, and blast AC/DC and Queen throughout the house. We see Jon Bon Jovi in concert and have the time of our lives. Most importantly, we create a bond that means the world to me. I call her Momma B. She's a lot of fun, and I really love her.

Barbara's time is being spent with her new boyfriend, and I feel the lack of her companionship. I want the attention and affection Barbara is getting too. She's so happy. I join an online dating website called Plenty of Fish. It's free, and I don't see the harm in meeting new people. What I don't know is that the only fish on the website are bloodthirsty piranhas. To say I'm desperate to be loved is an understatement.

Barbara doesn't approve of my risky choices and lets me know how she feels. Blaire and Ellie are over, and I feel it's safe to meet the man I've been talking to online with them there. The date makes the long drive to our house and parks in the laneway. I peek outside. Barbara, who I didn't know was going to be home, is standing behind me. "Oh, my gosh, Barbara. I can't look." I already regret my decision. He gets out of the car.

"What the hell were you thinking, Lainie?" Barbara asks. "Oh my God. He is way too old to be interested in a young woman like you." She shakes her head and shivers. "I don't want him in my house. Don't give out my address to any more strangers."

I feel embarrassed. I don't like being told no, but I know she's right. Blaire and Ellie come up the stairs and look at the short, balding guy approaching the front door. They look at me and, with plenty of swear words, ask me the same thing Barbara did.

"He doesn't look like his picture," I say, panicked. "I don't want to see him. I don't know what to do. He drove a long way to come and see me." I'm scared of my own shadow.

Blaire answers the door and tells the guy to get the hell off Barbara's property. "Go buy a toothbrush on your way home, you ——— bum! You look like you crush pop cans with your teeth!"

I'm sad the man's feelings are hurt but so relieved my brother was there to send him away.

The second stupid decision I make following the can-crushing-teeth guy is moving out of Barbara's house. The third bad decision is the relationship that follows.

I live in an apartment with Colton, my alcoholic boyfriend, who brings absolute chaos to my life, but also fun and adventure. I'm angry at myself for continually entering these relationships where abuse outweighs joy, arguments overtake peace, and sex surpasses love.

I hate who I am in these relationships. I create arguments to feel empowered, smart, and important. To be heard and listened to. I manipulate men to get what I need. *I want you to stay, so let me entice you with my body and charm.* I make boyfriends jealous by being overly friendly to men around me because I know it'll start a fight and I'll feel important and fought for. The men I attract love feeling big, so I make myself small, so they feel powerful.

I feel the need to care for broken men, serve them, and put their needs before mine, much like Mom. I put them on pedestals that should be kicked out from under them. I don't leave these controlling relationships, because I fear being unhoused, rejected, and abandoned, yet I stay in relationships and allow it all. I don't have a community to reach out to. I've burned bridges between me and my family. My pride keeps me from calling people to help, because I don't want to feel any more shame than I already do.

I'm sitting in my rusted black two-door Sunfire, staring at the doors of the church I ran out of as a fifteen-year-old child escaping the Thompson's. I moved to this small town as a thirteen-year-old-girl, full of hope and anticipation for new beginnings.

How did I get here?

I sang Christmas carols on the stage with my sisters while we shook bells in our hands. I prayed my heart out in the pews of its sanctuary for everyone but myself. I was an active member in our youth group and volunteered in the children's ministries. I gave 10 percent of my small earnings and loved feeling needed and accepted here. This building, at one point, felt like my second home.

Not tonight. Not anymore.

I pick up the pamphlet on my dash:

Celebrate Recovery.
A Christ-Centered 12 Step Recovery Program.
Healing your hurts, habits, and hang-ups.
A journey of real and lasting change.

It's been a long time, and I've been through a lot. *Does God still see me? Does he care about what I've been through?* I'm questioning his plan and the injustices of the world. I'm questioning my faith, the church, relationships, and organized religion. I'm questioning my life experiences and the purpose of it all.

I tap the pamphlet against the steering wheel, feeling hopeless and worried about the future. I snack from the bucket of emotions in my lap as memories play like short films in my mind. I feel haunted by the weight of shame and abandonment, which I carry on my back like a bag of old bones—rattling bones I've dug up in my deep, dark cave of regrets and mistakes. I keep coming back to this cave because it feels comfortable, but everything I desire is outside of its stone-cold walls. Belonging. Community. Love. Acceptance. Peace. I confuse familiarity of the past with feeling safe: working problems out on my own, putting others' needs before mine, and relying on myself to tend my broken heart. Living in chaos feels comfortable, but neglect never feels safe.

I don't even have enough gas in my car to get home. I'm parked between two yellow lines in the church's parking lot, facing a large green garbage bin. It reminds me of the cubby I used to hide in as a little girl. The Thompsons still attend this church, and Lisa is still the secretary. I have mixed feelings about being here again. Evening switches shifts with daylight and spreads its darkness all around me. I don't like being alone. I don't like feeling alone either. I lean my head back against the headrest. The church lights behind me reflect from the rearview mirror and into my pooling eyes. I breathe deeply and drop my forehead to the steering wheel to cry.

You can do this. You have nothing left to lose.

I swipe the tears from under my tired eyes and toss the recovery pamphlet back onto my dashboard. I push against my car's creaking door and get out. I stand for a moment in the brisk evening wind, staring at the church building. *You need this*, I tell my weary heart.

I enter the church and look around. I smile when I see the warm, familiar face of Milli, an older woman who still attends the church. I feel no judgment from her and breathe a sigh of relief. She wraps me in an embrace and leads me to the sanctuary, where I sit silently by myself to reflect.

After a few minutes, a longtime church member introduces the twelve-step recovery program and reads the Serenity Prayer:

"God, grant me the serenity to accept the things I cannot change, the courage to change the things I can, and the wisdom to know the difference."

I've heard this before but never applied it to my life.

The leader continues: "Living one day at a time, enjoying one moment at a time; accepting hardship as a pathway to peace; taking, as Jesus did, this sinful world as it is, not as I would have it; trusting that you will make all things right if I surrender to your will; so that I may be reasonably happy in this life and supremely happy with you forever in the next. Amen."

I've never heard the last part of the Serenity Prayer before. I read the whole prayer again. "… Accept the things I cannot change." "Change" resonates with me, but the word "accept?" How am I supposed to do that when I still feel so angry at myself and other people? I know I can't change my past, no matter how badly I wish I can. I don't even want to think about the impossible task of unraveling the layers of mistakes I've made. I'm not proud of my decisions in life, and there doesn't seem to be enough bleach in the world to clean the stains of shame I'm covered in.

Music begins to play, and we're invited to stand together. There's a vulnerability and closeness I feel to God when I sing, but these songs they're playing about forgiveness, surrender, joy in sorrow, and praising God in all storms of life feels too hard to sing right now. I'm not ready to forgive anyone yet, and I certainly don't feel joy. I won't even allow the words to leave my mouth. They're not true to me. Not yet. Bitterness rises from my gut, and a surging heat takes over my body. I feel dizzy and sick. I sit down to steady myself. Tears fall to the old carpet between my feet as I wrestle with God. My hair dangles forward like a closing curtain, protecting me from being seen so vulnerable.

God, where have you been? Are you hiding from me? Do you not see me here suffering? Have I not suffered enough? What is it that you want from me? What more can I give? Everything is gone.

I feel like your human pin cushion with this heavy life you've cursed me with. What do I have to do to feel accepted and loved by you? Where do I belong in this unpredictable world of pain and disappointment? God, I feel so alone. I don't feel you close to me anymore.

What's the point of my life? What is there to live for? Who would stay for someone with nothing to offer? I feel like a burden. God, I'm so confused about who you are. I want to lay down my deepest pain, but I need to know I can trust you. I need to know your promises are true. I need a way out of this. I can't live like this anymore.

When the songs finish, the leader discusses the step we're on, says a prayer, then dismisses us into small groups. I like that the men are in a separate room, away from us. I'm not sure what to think of being the youngest girl here. Most of the women are old enough to be my mother, and some, my grandmother. Our group leader asks us to go around the circle and introduce ourselves, briefly mentioning why we've decided to join the group.

"Would you like to start?" she says, opening her four fingers toward me while gripping a pen with her thumb.

"Uh, hi," I start awkwardly. "I'm Lainie."

And just like in the movies, the other women respond in unison: "Hi, Lainie. This is a safe space."

I laugh and look around the circle at their eager and interested faces. "You're not going to say that every time I talk, right?"

"This is a safe space," the leader repeats. The others nod. "Begin when you're ready."

Okay, then. I concentrate on my breathing and give myself a moment to gather my thoughts before beginning. "We're all afraid of being judged, right? If we look like we have it all together on the outside, no one pries or asks us hard questions about what's really going on in our lives."

Exposing my deepest pain to people I don't know feels dangerous. "Judgment-free zones." I scoff. "I mean, is there really such a thing?"

My throat tightens up, and tears start to form. The women look at me as if they understand, and they wait for me to continue. I really want to go last, to hear everyone else's stories first to determine how much I should share. I decide to let it all out.

"I grew up in a crime-filled, impoverished area in Toronto with my mentally ill mother, and several of my siblings. Mom had nine children but was mentally incapable of raising them. Mom had me placed in foster care twice when I was young, and then, when I was almost nine, she made a phone call from a motel payphone, without me knowing, and asked relatives to come and get me. I was stripped from her leg that day and never returned to live with her again. Being torn from her and my family was the most excruciating experience of my life. I feel unlovable, unworthy, and disposable. My mother was very neglectful toward my needs. I've never fully processed what's happened to me."

"I have a foggy vision of what love is. From what I've seen and experienced in my life, love hurts and must be earned. The pain I drag behind me is a shadow I can't let go of. It covers me anytime I feel joy and convinces me it's a hug. It's an enemy I've always known, and for some reason, I've made friends with it. I hate myself for believing I deserve pain as punishment. I want to feel like a missing puzzle piece discovered in someone's pocket, happy to be found— to finally have a place I know I belong. I don't know if that'll ever happen for me."

I continue. "I don't know who I am when I'm alone, and that scares me. I don't feel I have anything left in me to offer anyone anymore. I don't feel I'm worth anything without the validation of others. I don't know what it's like to be me or what my purpose is in life. I just want the pain to end. I hate who I've become."

I begin sobbing uncontrollably and decide to end there. I briefly look up into the eyes of the women around the circle, trying to figure out whether what I said was okay. *Did I even answer the question?* I'm highly empathetic and don't want my story to hurt anyone's feelings. I'm shocked to see the other women crying too.

Our leader reminds the group not to jump in for hugs, rub a person's back who's sharing, or even to respond with words. We are to let the person process and feel her emotions by herself. It feels weird to cry alone. To avoid the awkwardness, I excuse myself to the bathroom so I can splash my face with cool water and catch my breath. I don't want to miss anyone's story, so I quickly return to the group and listen as they share. I'm amazed. These women are walking, talking, living miracles. They speak of addictions, mental health struggles, abuse, trauma, anger, devastating loss, and grief.

I've never seen a psychologist or paid to see a therapist, so I don't have any official diagnosis, but what I do know is that while our pain may be different, our tears all fall the same.

After everyone shares, we go back upstairs to the sanctuary and read the Serenity Prayer again. We sing a few more songs before closing and are given workbooks containing questions to go through at home. I want to commit to finishing the program. Before I leave for the night, a woman I don't know approaches me with a white envelope. My name is written across it, and I can feel something hard inside. "God told me to give this to you. God bless you and your journey, Lainie. See you next week."

I thank her for the card and exit the building to sit in my car. I rip the envelope open and see a fifty-dollar gift card to the gas station down the road. I can't believe it. I rest my forehead on my steering wheel and smile. I thank God for showing up and giving me a glimmer of hope. This whole night feels like a warm, loving embrace from God.

My eyes look swollen, and my body feels weak from being drained of the heaviness I carried into tonight. I keep begging broken people to give me something they don't have. Pain is a vicious cycle; hurt people hurt people, but I believe it's possible that healed people heal people too. I can't keep holding on to the anger, hate, and resentment I feel toward myself, others, and God.

For the first time in a long time, I pray.

"God, thank you for the hope I felt tonight. You gave me this life for a reason. I'm struggling to feel how any good might come from what you've allowed. If you didn't give me this life to hurt me, then what is the greater purpose of it all? I am exhausted from life's battles, and I can't keep fighting alone. I need you. I need you to transform my life into something meaningful. The Bible says the enemy intended to harm me but you intended it all for good. Show me that it's true. Show me who you are. Reintroduce me to Jesus—not the Jesus I was taught to be afraid of, but the God who says he loved me so much he gave his life for me. The one who says he is close to the brokenhearted and who feels my pain as if it were his own. The God who weeps with me. That is the God I need right now."

CHAPTER EIGHTEEN

The Simmonses

2006

After completing the twelve steps of recovery, I put an ad in the church's bulletin for a young woman looking for a room to rent, and to my surprise, someone responds rather quickly.

Hanna and Gus Simmons have offered me the opportunity to live with them, and I'm beyond grateful. I input their address into my phone and begin to make the trip. They live in the middle of nowhere. I travel country road after country road. Farmer's fields. Horses. Cows. No one is around. I check the address again when I pull into their laneway because I can't believe it's the right house. It's a custom-built home that sits on a dreamy hundred acres of never-ending forest. I can heal here. There is a beautiful wooden-arched bridge that leads to a secluded island in the middle of a pond. On the island is a big old tree that offers rest beneath its branches; this is a place to enjoy the beauty of God's sunsets. God has shown up for me in a huge way. To make things even better, the people who live here are even more beautiful than the property.

Hanna is Hungarian and can cook unlike anyone I have ever met. I love spending time with her in the kitchen while I watch her prepare meals from scratch. She even makes her own noodles by hand. She teaches me so much and is the woman-figure I need in my life right now. She works so hard. Her husband, Gus, is a lumberjack by day and an antique tradesman by night. He is good at everything he does, especially negotiating and bargaining deals. He knows the incredible values of things I would probably throw away, such as old paintings he sells online for jaw-dropping amounts.

Gus wants to show me how to shoot a rifle. I'm both excited and terrified. He quickly takes a shot, then hands the gun to me. I pick it up, pull it into my shoulder, and look through the scope. I steady the gun, aim it at the Styrofoam target, and wait. And wait. And wait. I can't muster up the bravery to pull the trigger. I worry it'll blow my arm off or I'll put a hole through the roof. I'm taking too long, and Gus can't handle the waiting. In three seconds flat, Gus puts his cigarette back into his mouth, snatches the gun from my hands, and shoots the Buck target hundreds of yards away right through its chest. My heart races. I decline trying again. Shooting guns is not for me.

* * *

The fiery, fading sunset peeks through Hanna and Gus's wintry forest and dances along the spines of drooping icicles. I find it quite amazing how the sun, in its perfect timing, transforms what is lonely and lifeless into a vibrant community of rainbow-dancing crystals. I absorb its view, deep in thought. I want to shine radiantly too, even if it's only for a few minutes. Little do I know that the light I need will soon be walking out of the forest.

Gus is at the kitchen table drinking homogenized whole milk, enjoying the clear view of his land from the large dining room windows. My sister, Rosie, who is visiting for the night, sits beside me on a tall-backed barstool, watching Hanna prepare her famous chili for dinner. We rest our elbows on the cold granite countertops with our hands under our chins. There's a big blue truck parked along the curve of the laneway.

"Whose vehicle is parked out there?" I ask.

"Levi's out hunting for deer," Gus says. "You'll like him, Lainie. He's a good guy." Gus puts his milk glass down and smirks at Hanna. She looks up over her glasses at Gus, who has milk in his mustache. Her full cheeks lift all the way up, exposing her small, thin-lipped smile.

"Hanna, what are you smiling about?" I ask, smiling too.

"Oh, nothing …" she sings. Her shoulders bounce up and down as she laughs. "He's a hard worker. Smart boy." She gives the chili a stir. "Lives with his parents, our good friends, down the road. He's a cutie-pie. A good-looking, nice young man."

"What are you two conjuring up?" I pry. "I'm not interested. I just broke up with that wingnut of a guy."

"Who, Colton?" Rosie laughs. "He was so funny, but he was definitely insane."

"He pulled my sparkplugs so I couldn't leave him, then put my car in the demolition derby."

"You sure know how to pick 'em." Rosie laughs again.

"Levi would never do something like that." Hanna says, getting us back on track.

I grab the binoculars from the dining room window ledge to look through the trees.

"What kind of guy sits in a tree stand that high up from the ground, freezing his arse off in the middle of winter, trying to kill Bambi?" I blurt out. "It doesn't make any sense."

"Probably as much sense as a girl holding a pair of binoculars looking out to the trees for a man she's not interested in," Gus snaps back. Touché, Gus.

Later, as the sky begins to darken, Rosie and I are setting the table for dinner when Gus gets up from his chair and opens the patio door.

"Levi! Come inside and warm up with some chili. We want you to meet someone!"

I panic. "Gus! You *didn't!*"

"You're gonna need another place setting, dear," he laughs.

My heart is racing. Levi walks in, and my eyes bulge from their sockets. I can't help but stare. He's almost six feet tall and is of a medium build, with wavy light brown hair and a manicured beard. He has gorgeous hazel eyes and a straight-toothed, one-sided smile I find incredibly attractive.

"Chili's hot," Hanna says.

He's hotter. I grab Rosie by the shoulders.

"Hi. This is my sister Rosie."

"And what's your name?" he asks.

"Oh, yeah. Sorry. I'm Lainie. This is my sister Rosie."

You said that already.

"You said that already," Hanna says, looking over her glasses. Her shoulders bounce up and down again. "Sit down, sweetie. Let's eat."

CHAPTER NINETEEN

Hearts in My Eyes

2006

Levi's family is coming over for a Christmas party tonight. I'm elated to see Levi again and meet his family. My stomach is filled with butterflies, and my heart is fluttering about in my chest. I spend hours getting myself ready, and help Hanna prepare the food and decorations. Everything looks perfect.

I greet Levi's mom, Maggie, with a hug, and introduce myself, then say hello to his dad, Manuel, and introduce myself again. I welcome his older sister, Maria, and his two younger brothers, José and William, into the house and offer to take their coats. When Levi enters the house, my whole face flushes red. I quickly walk into Hanna's bedroom to throw the coats on her bed. Before leaving the room, I fluff my hair, critique my makeup, and fix my outfit. I walk toward Levi and flash him the smile I've been practicing. He smiles too and opens his arms for a friendly hug.

"It's nice to see you again," I say.

"It's nice to see you too, Lainie."

Over the next few hours, I find myself mesmerized by the way his family interacts with each other. Their love is louder than the laughter in the room and echoes within the halls. They invite me into their circle of joy, and it feels good. The evening is full of delicious food and hilarious games while NHL hockey plays on the TV in the background.

Levi and I get partnered for a jelly bean toss competition and win. Hanna awards us our prize—an oversize white candle on a black pillar with fake greenery. Levi willingly lets me keep it. Levi and his siblings share memories of their childhood throughout the night, giving their own versions of what really happened. Gus and Manuel talk about the dart league they're in. Maggie and Hanna converse while observing everyone in the room—especially me and Levi.

Hanna hands out a couple of gifts under her tree for Levi's parents and their kids. I feel awkward. I cross my arms and legs and twist my ankles together beneath my chair. Levi's family isn't my own; neither are the Simmonses. *I need out of here.* Levi puts his arm around the back of my chair, and suddenly I no longer want to run away. Hanna passes me a gift with a wink, as if to say, "You're exactly where you're meant to be, Lainie." It means so much.

Everyone is tired from a great evening together and packs up for home. Levi wants to visit with me a while longer and asks Gus and Hanna if it's okay. Butterflies swarm throughout my entire inner being and escape through my eyelashes. The soft glow of the Christmas tree lights shines in the background as I begin to tell Levi how much fun I've had with him and his family tonight and how much the night has meant to me.

"I love seeing you with your family. It's easy to see how much you all love each other. You're all so happy."

Levi looks at me sideways. "I don't know what you mean. We're just a regular family."

"You're not just a regular family, Levi. You're the family I dreamed of having."

"We fight all the time. Trust me."

"So does my family. You've had your whole lives together, though. You laugh together about your childhoods in a way that shows you felt safe. My family laughs together too, but you'd think we were mentally twisted for the things we find funny." I laugh. "It's beautiful to see a family like yours. I've dreamed of it my entire life."

"Okay ..." Levi says, trying to make sense of my layered thinking.

"Sorry," I laugh. "Keep going. Tell me more about you."

Levi explains how he was raised in an incredible Christian home with parents who deeply love each other. His parents run a successful catering company. *An unlimited supply of food … this is good.* He and his siblings have benefited from private Christian education for both elementary and secondary school and have all played on several sports teams. *They must be rich.* It seems as if Levi's never been without anything in his life. He says his life is very simple, that he doesn't live in a fancy house or drive fancy cars, and he doesn't consider his family to be well-off. For a girl who's come from the streets, I quietly disagree.

"What's your family like?" he asks.

Oh, that dreaded question. I figure I have two choices: I can either scare him off right away by telling this story honestly, before there's an attachment, or I can avoid the truth, wait until feelings are involved, and hope for the best. *I can't be enough for a guy like you, Levi.* I hush my mind and decide to be honest.

Levi rubs his forehead. "I had no idea. I never would have guessed. I'm sorry you had to go through all that," he says, putting his hand on my knee. The warmth of his touch sends a tingle up my spine. He's not sure what else to say. It's a lot for anyone to take in. I put my hand over his and squeeze it. "Thanks for listening. I know it's a lot. Sorry."

"It's okay," he responds. "I feel bad for sharing my privilege when you've lived that way."

"I'm glad you lived the life you did, Levi. I mean, I don't know you that well, but I think you turned out okay," I say with a wink. We both laugh. "I'm glad you went first," I joke. "You probably wouldn't be sitting here if I had started."

"Maybe not," he laughs. "Just kidding, of course I would. That stuff doesn't scare me."

I feel a connection to Levi, and from what I can tell, he feels the same. He's a deep breath of fresh air. I'm incredibly blessed to have met him, even if nothing comes of this. He's nineteen years old, seems to have his life together, and (gasp) also has goals and dreams for his future. He's a junior horticulture student in college and plans to own his own landscaping business one day.

A couple hours of conversation pass, and Hanna yells from

upstairs that Levi should probably head home soon. We switch phone numbers before I walk him upstairs and say good night. I close the door behind him and whisper to Hanna that she was right. She giggles and says, "I told you so." I run down to my room, punch the air, and jump up and down as if I just won the lottery. How is it possible to be this excited over someone I just met? I crawl into bed and straighten my duvet cover around my body as though I have my life together or something. I look up to the ceiling and smile like a horse. I grip my phone as if it's about to sprout wings and fly away, and hope for a message from him. "God, thank you."

My flip phone pings with a notification alert. I'm so excited I nearly flick the top right off and send it flying across the room. A message reads, "Good night, beautiful. I'd love to see you again."

I bite my duvet while I type back, "Good night, handsome. I'd love that too."

* * *

We pull into the parking lot of East Side Mario's, a restaurant known for its pasta and bottomless salads. We're seated at a wooden table with wooden legs. I prefer sitting in a booth, but I won't ask otherwise. It's only our first date, after all. I joke that food is my love language, but it's a huge insecurity and slight obsession. I really want to order a massive plate of pasta, a big, juicy steak with mashed potatoes smothered in gravy, a bottomless Caesar salad, and six warm buttered buns. Instead I order a small Caesar salad and a small side of french fries. Levi asks why I ordered so little, and I lie and say I'm not that hungry. The truth is, I don't want him spending too much money on me. I use a fork and knife to cut my fries and salad to look proper. I have a better chance of the food making it into my mouth that way. My thoughts and feelings are distracting, and my nerves have invited all their friends to a house party in my body. Who cuts fries and an already chopped salad? We share more about our lives and laugh until our meals are finished. The waiter presents the dessert menu. Levi kindly declines and mentions he has a special place he'd like to take me.

I feel silly for ordering what I did for dinner. I also feel rude for convincing Levi that the fancy dessert place he really wants to take me to is too expensive and that a dollar ice-cream cone from McDonald's would be fine. I don't feel I deserve to be spoiled with expensive desserts.

Victoria Park in downtown London is my new favorite place to be during the Christmas season. Tonight feels like a private invitation into a gently shaken snow globe. I breathe in the crisp, magical evening air and smile. Everything feels right. Snow blankets the frozen ground on either side of the crunchy, salted path we're walking on. I'm in heels, but I don't care, and if I can't walk tomorrow, I won't tell anyone. Couples in love pass us as they walk hand in hand with their warm drinks and smiling faces. Levi reaches for my hand and pulls me close too. We talk about school, our futures, our goals, and our dreams. Classic Christmas carols fill the few quiet moments between conversation. I hum along as I admire the fully decorated trees, crowded with thousands of twinkling, colorful lights, and the hand-painted wooden Christmas displays around the park. We end our walk near the large outdoor skating rink packed with people of all ages and abilities showcasing their talents.

We finish our walk together and grab a warm drink from the local café to enjoy on the ride home. Levi opens the car door for me and, when I'm settled, closes it gently. When we arrive home, he walks me to my door. No one's ever done this before. I reach for the cold metal handle and turn to face him. I beg my subconscious to take a mental picture of his beautiful features so I can dream about them tonight. Levi's hands are buried deep in his pockets, and his elbows are nervously swaying back and forth. I let go of the door handle and reach inside his open coat to wrap my arms around his back. I lean my head back and push myself up onto my tiptoes for a kiss he gladly accepts. He wraps me in a tight embrace and holds me for a moment.

"So, does this make us official?" he asks.

"I'd love that," I whisper. I gaze up into his safe, peaceful eyes and see the reflection of the night's stars.

He tucks my hair behind my ears. "I was hoping you'd say that."

He gently kisses my lips again. "I should probably go." I thank him for the most wonderful evening and for making me feel so special. "Of course. You deserve it," he says, before saying good night and walking away.

I run downstairs to my room and trust my bed to catch my fall as I replay Levi's words in my head over and over again.

"You deserve it."

I will learn many positive and negative things about myself over the next four years of dating Levi. Each year will be filled with lessons of love, pain, hope, and self-discovery. Levi isn't afraid to tell me about the good, bad, and ugly parts of who I am. I'm certainly not afraid to do the same. He calls me out on my lack of attachment, stubbornness, impatience, anger, distrust in people, and fears and anxieties. I'm jealous that Levi has lived such a wonderful life, and I struggle with feeling worthy of him because of the stink of my past. I cry and scream that he'll never be able to understand me or figure me out. He listens to me and continually shows patience, even when I lose it all myself. I'm frustrated by not knowing how to love Levi properly, and I'm frustrated with myself for not letting him love me. He deserves what I'm incapable of giving, and I'm deserving of what he offers me. I don't know how to love myself, and it's showing.

I give Levi every reason to leave me. I push him away when things are hard, but he pulls me closer. I shut him out with the silent treatment, but he chooses to sit in the still, dead air beside me. When I'm defensive and protective, he shows me he's safe and trustworthy. I reject his affection, but he patiently waits for me to come back to him. I'm stubborn and run from painful conversations, but he pursues me and works things out. He encourages me to push forward when I want to stay where I'm comfortable. I have tested his loyalty and know he's struggling with our relationship. I want to know how far he'll go to fight for me when things are hard. I selfishly hurt him to make him feel the same pain I struggle through daily. It's not fair to him, and I don't want to do it anymore.

Levi is exhausted from the fighting. He looks defeated. "Why won't you let me love you?" he asks, on the verge of tears. His question cuts me deep. My behavior is humiliating. My pain is too heavy to carry, and I've been throwing it all onto his back. I don't want to watch him suffer anymore. Removing my armor and surrendering my heart to love feels too dangerous. I've had to protect every part of myself for so many years. Levi has no desire to control me. I fight so hard to resist him, yet he's all I want. Peace feels like an impossible task for someone who has known only chaos.

Levi is stable, steadfast, and consistent, even when he's hurting. He recognizes my potential, encourages me to be the best version of myself, and pushes me past the excuses I make for not trying to move forward in my life. He nudges me out of my comfort zone, where I feel vulnerable and scared. I don't believe in who I am yet, but he's helping me get there.

Levi and I have one intense conversation—or passionate argument, rather—which shatters the tough exterior I hide behind and exposes the bare and tender parts of both our hearts. Levi's relationship with God is first and foremost in his life. He's made a commitment to God to wait until marriage to be sexually intimate. I'm caught in a jealousy battle between God, me, and Levi. The act of being intimate, to me, means I'm being loved. It's what I was used for in past relationships. It's the act that makes me feel worthy again after an argument and how I know I've been forgiven or accepted again. It's a way to have a clean slate and start over again when things are difficult. My perception of love is wrong, but I don't know it yet. I hate the feeling of being rejected or not good enough. My desire to get what I want, because of the jealousy I hold against his commitment to God, has me more determined to get my way.

I do what I always do when I'm hurt: I slice him with my words. I give him ultimatums. For the first time, I make him cry. The silence hanging between us speaks so many words. I've finally broken him and pushed him too far. He's angry, and I know I deserve whatever he's about to say. With tears in his eyes, he yells at me.

"Has no one ever loved you properly? Has no one ever made you feel like you're worth waiting for? Has no one ever told you no?" I want to hold him and apologize, but he's too hurt and won't accept it. The pain in his voice is unbearable. "Lainie, I love you like I should. Even when you make it seem impossible. I know you're worth waiting for. Why can't you see that about yourself? I'm going to continue to tell you no. I made a commitment to God, and I'm honoring it. I can't wait to marry you, but you can't treat me like this anymore."

My walls have crumbled to the ground, and my soul is laid bare at his feet.

I want him to hold me as I cry, but I don't deserve his affection after the way I've treated him.

I wipe my tears away with my sleeve and look into his hazel eyes. "Why would you want to wait for someone like me?"

"I see you for who you are, Lainie. You're worth more than the men in your life have shown you. You're more than your beauty. You're more than just sex. I want a relationship with you that will last forever, but I can't have you constantly bullying me and making me feel like less of a man."

"I'm sorry, Levi," I cry. "I don't know how to love you properly. I need you to show me how."

"I will if you let me."

Levi pulls me close, and I nestle into the safety of his arms.

I feel vulnerable and exposed, yet I've never felt safer. For the first time in my life, I experience what true love feels like. All I want to do is make Levi feel this way too.

‎ ⁜

CHAPTER TWENTY

Mom's Apartment

SUMMER 2008

The sun aims its fiery rays at my fair, freckled skin, which sizzles like butter in a skillet when in direct sunlight. I'm out for a run, trying to clear my mind, but worry is dancing on my heart with nails in its shoes. I have this overwhelming feeling something is wrong with Mom, and I can't shake the feeling she's in danger. God is connecting the lines between me and my mother, and I don't know why. She lives an hour and a half from me. I decide the heat must be getting to me.

I round the street corner to my one-bedroom second-story apartment above a little diner called Salt and Peppers. I can smell the swirling aromas of freshly made soups and breads ascending toward my place. I push the door open with my hip and slog up each step of the staircase. I walk in, kick my shoes off, and welcome the embrace from the air conditioning. The sweaty outlines of my socks leave a trail behind me as I walk across the cool floor to the fridge. I pour myself a large glass of water and hope it'll quench my thirst and help me think more clearly.

I call Ellie and tell her about my distressing thoughts about Mom. She agrees we should make the trip to Stratford to check in on her, but Ellie doesn't drive yet, and I don't want to. I'm anxious. I know my quick heart rate and sweaty hands aren't just from running. I call Levi, whom I've been dating for a year and a half, and tell him about the aching pit in my stomach.

"Do you want me to drive you there to make sure she's okay?" I can feel the pulse in my face. "Uh …" I begin. I'm hesitant. I'm not sure I'm ready for him to meet her yet. Levi understands Mom has a mental illness and consistently reassures me that meeting her won't change the way he feels about me; I'm sure it will. Exposing Levi to my past is both my greatest fear and deepest desire.

"Are you sure you're ready to meet her?" I ask, offering him a chance to change his mind. "I've spent years witnessing strangers' glares and hearing their rude comments. She still lives the same way we did when I was a child. She can't take care of herself, Levi. Or her place. It's embarrassing. I'm worried you'll think differently of me when you meet her."

"I've told you a million times, you don't have to worry about that with me. I'm ready to meet her whenever you're comfortable enough to introduce me."

"I know, I'm just protective of her. Everything about her is different. She doesn't live like a normal person."

"I think you're protecting yourself, Lainie, not your mom. No offense. No one else is worried about me meeting her except you."

I'm offended by his response but know he's right. Levi has a way of seeing right through me. His honesty, not sugar-coating my excuses, is one of the many things I love about him. I'm regretful of my past and the stain it's left on me. I'm building a new life and reputation, independent from my past, and I don't want to see it crumble to the ground. I feel protective of myself and my relationship.

I'm still healing from my mother's mistakes and recovering from the damage her decisions have caused me. Our unresolved issues are like bulging suitcases filled with dirty laundry. They explode with a single touch. I'm not protecting my mother from Levi; I'm protecting myself from my mother. The fear I have of the past is debilitating, and I don't ever want to go back. The way my mother looks and lives transports me right back to feeling neglected, unsafe, and scared. I don't want to expose those deep, unhealed places to Levi any more than I already have.

I act as though I have my life together and do a good job at pretending my past doesn't exist. I work hard, have my own apartment, and pay my own bills. I'm strong-willed, independent, and educated. I take care of myself physically and have a big personality; I have a lot of friends, and I'm full of joy when I'm around others. I use my humor, appearance, and quick wit as a shield to guard against people asking me tough questions, the kind that requires the truth. I constantly strive for perfection and validation from others and live for their approval. Not many people know about the dirty, pained, and abandoned little girl living within me: the one with the lice-infested bowl-cut and urine-stained clothes who spent her evenings knocking on doors begging for food—the girl who is ever-present within but inaccessible to others.

Mom's mental state is fragile, and I'm not sure how she'll take meeting Levi. She's been betrayed by men most of her life and has no desire to be around them anymore. The only men she allows in her life are her grown sons who love and protect her. I know Mom is going to ask Levi humiliating, paranoid questions and shoot him the dirtiest of looks. I mean, if looks could kill …

"Don't make eye contact with her for too long." I explain. "And don't tell jokes either. She takes everything literally and doesn't understand them. Oh, and don't say anything she can twist into thinking negatively. She doesn't trust men." I continue to warn him.

Levi is getting frustrated. "Lainie … Please. Stop."

"Sorry, I want you to be prepared." I've never introduced a man to her before. "This is a big deal for me, Levi. She doesn't like men, and I don't want her to be mean to you."

"I think I can handle it, honey."

"Sorry, I'm nervous. Just promise you'll still love me tomorrow."

Levi squeezes my hand to reassure me. "I'll love you tomorrow no matter what happens today, okay?"

We arrive outside Mom's building and see flashing fire trucks and ambulances blocking traffic. Residents are outside, swarming the place. An instant shockwave of panic rushes through my veins.

God, you knew I was supposed to be here today. Tell me my mother's okay.

We see Carlos out front, Mom's neighbor who lives across the hall. His skin is weathered, his eyes are lost, and his voice is soothing and kind. He's drunk, as usual, sitting on the old wooden bench he claims outside his run-down complex. His shirt is unbuttoned, displaying his curly gray chest hair. His cane is resting on his bouncing leg, and five or six crushed Busch beer cans lie around his dirty, worn-out shoes. He stands up and slurs his speech. I can barely see his lips moving under his nicotine-stained mustache. He says he watches out for Mom and helps protect her from the delirious people in the building. We ask him whether he's seen Mom, and he casually informs us that her apartment has caught fire and he doesn't know where she is.

I approach the firemen who are done inside and packing up to leave. I question them about what happened. They tell us apartment number ten caught fire, but it was empty at the time, and no one was hurt.

That's Mom's apartment. Where's my mom?

There are only three places she goes: Giant Tiger, her favorite place to shop; Swiss Chalet, her favorite place to eat; and the pond, her favorite place to watch the swans and geese. I spot her walking down the road toward us and can't help but think she looks like Big Bird gone goth. Her skin looks as if it's never seen the sun. She's wearing a bumble bee–yellow teased-out wig that stands out a foot on each side of her head. It's a scorching hot day, and Mom's wearing a big, gorilla-like black fur coat, loosely buttoned down the center with leather loops and wooden buttons. I can see she's topless underneath because her sagging boobs are swaying, and her nipples are playing peek-a-boo. She refuses to wear a bra or underwear, and her old, worn-out jeans are skin-tight and pulled too high.

Her makeup—oh, her makeup. Her beautiful green eyes are trapped inside dark, deep caves of black. Her eyelids are colored with blue and green Crayola markers, right up to her colored-in black eyebrows. She's reapplied to her short lashes her chunky black mascara, which has clumped and smudged. Thick streaks of black eyeliner coat her eyelids, and multiple layers of black lipstick, from the dollar store, have been applied continually. She presses her lips tightly together and vigorously swipes the flattened lipstick back and forth across her lips, not caring about it being smeared outside the lip lines. She's also added a small vertical line of black eyeliner beneath her bottom lip toward her chin and dotted a black beauty mark on her left cheek to resemble Marilyn Monroe. With her smooth, light skin, it really pops.

Mom is both curious and confused by the commotion happening outside her place. She's even more confused to see me, Levi, and Ellie standing in front of her building as she approaches us.

"Oh, Lainie and Ellie. I didn't know you were coming today."

"Hi, Mom, this is my boyfriend, Levi."

"Hi, Annie," Levi says.

Mom makes brief eye contact with Levi, scoffs, then quickly looks away from him. "Hi," is all she offers back. "That's nice you guys drove all the way to come and see me. Why are there fire trucks here? Are they here for me?"

I turn to Levi and Ellie. "I knew something was wrong today. I swear. I knew we were supposed to be here. I felt it."

"Really?" Mom laughs. "I have those feelings sometimes too. It's nice to see you all though. I just went out for a walk to the store to get a few things, some Pepsi, and some chips. Wanna come upstairs for a visit? Away from all these deranged people?"

I laugh at the irony.

"Mom, there was a big fire in your apartment."

Mom raises her eyebrows slightly. "Oh, really? Can you come up for a visit anyway? All the delusional people are outside," she repeats herself.

There's no panic in Mom's voice. No alarm. She isn't scared. No hand gestures. Barely any questioning. She's just happy we're here and wants to spend time with us. After the fire trucks leave, the residents are granted entry to the building. We bring Mom up to her apartment.

"Oh, wow. Did someone paint my apartment black?" she asks, looking up and pointing to the ceiling.

"Apparently you did, Mom. Charcoal. You almost burnt your place down."

"Hmm." She huffs, looking around.

She really doesn't understand what she's done.

"What happened here, Mom? The firefighters said they found a candle on the stove."

"Oh, yeah. The apartment was kind of stinky. The clothes have been in the bathtub for a few days. I wanted the apartment to smell nice, so I put a candle on the burner and left to go get some snacks. I guess I forgot to shut the stove off."

Levi, Ellie, and I have much bigger concerns than the burnt walls. The air is heavy, and the stench is intense. I want to plug my nose, but I don't want to inhale through my mouth either. We look left to the bathroom. Grime is thick everywhere. The stink from the wet clothes soaking in the bathtub almost makes me retch. I reminisce about the childhood places we lived that looked and smelled just like this.

"Mom, they have a washer and dryer downstairs you can use. Why don't you use them?"

"No. I like doing my laundry in the bathtub. There's a lot of creepy people downstairs who use that laundry room."

I'm baffled at the way her brain works. She doesn't consider this creepy at all.

Mom believes her looks and her lifestyle are totally normal. She has no idea what society's norms are, nor does she care. She doesn't believe she dresses strangely, nor does she know her makeup scares people. She believes she is Marilyn Monroe reincarnated. In her eyes, everyone else has the problem. She stops and laughs at people in public while pointing her finger in their direction like a child. She says things like, "Look at that weird lady's pink hair!" I respond, "Mom, that's not very nice. Maybe she thinks you look weird." Mom quickly scoffs in disbelief and says, "I'm beautiful. No one thinks that." Another time, while out at Swiss Chalet, she pointed to a table of Mennonites and laughed, saying, "Look at those funny-looking Pilgrims!" It still makes me laugh; she is so vain, and so unaware of social etiquette.

Straight ahead is Mom's bedroom, the only bedroom in the apartment. I try to push open the door but realize it has furniture behind it. "That's the cat's room. I wanted him to have the bed. He likes it there."

"The cat's room? You're not sleeping in your bedroom?"

"No. That's okay, though; I just sleep on the couch."

"Mom, why does the cat get your bedroom?"

"I just think Mr. Precious should have his own room."

I don't know what to think. Should I be more concerned that she thinks her cat needs the bedroom to itself (with no litter box) or that she lives like this? It breaks my heart. She's lived this way most of her life. I lived this way with her. I use my shoulders to push past the barricade behind the door and open it enough to fit through. Mom's feral tabby cat, full of terror (and smoke inhalation), races out of the apartment. I follow him down the hall, down the stairs, and into the bottom of the stairwell, where he's cornered himself. I try making kissing noises while rubbing my fingers together as if I have food, but he isn't buying it. With the way he is hissing and clawing at me, I decide against it and make a call to the local humane society to pick him up instead.

To the right of the bedroom is a small living room with an even smaller kitchen attached to it. *You have got to be kidding me.* I wouldn't let an animal live like this. A heavy comforter covers her living room window, leaving the place almost black. I remove the blanket from the window, knowing it'll upset Mom, and open the small window.

Dust covers everything in the living room, including nine plastic dolls Mom has lined up in a row, each one representing one of her children. She proudly points down the row, naming all her children while explaining how much the dolls look like us. They look like they belong in a horror movie. I sit beside Mom on the couch and notice red sores on the nape of her neck and little black bugs scrambling from beneath her wig. The bugs from the infested couch she sleeps on every night are snacking on her body. She has red patches all over her pale skin. Ellie, who has chosen to stand, starts to cry when she sees Mom's skin. I get up to hug her and cry too. Levi is far beyond his comfort zone and isn't sure what to do to help.

Mom is used to living this way, and it doesn't seem to bother her at all. She insists everything is okay and reiterates that we don't need to worry about her. I feel so many emotions: anger, frustration, sadness, and confusion. I don't know what to do or how to help her.

The little kitchen still has the candlestick on the stove, reminding me again of Mom's inability to care for herself. There is garbage on the floors and counter, and the fridge is empty except for a couple cans of Pepsi, a bottle of ketchup, and a stick of butter. I wouldn't wish this life on anyone.

Mom loves buying fast food and eating at restaurants, but when she runs out of money, she goes to the food bank. She makes simple dishes like spaghetti, stovetop lasagna, ramen noodles, boxed macaroni and cheese, chili con carne, and, of course, potatoes and onions.

The three of us leave the apartment to talk, leaving my mom on the couch upstairs. We need to breathe fresh air. Mom is going to die here alone if we don't do something immediately. We call Rachel first, then the rest of our siblings, to let them know what's happened and to ask what we should do. We all know Mom can't continue life this way. We go back upstairs to talk to Mom about getting help, but she's resistant and stubborn. She won't leave her apartment or take any of our advice.

Levi, Ellie, and I clean Mom's place as best we can and head home for the night. I have guilt in my soul, pain in my heart, and a mind full of questions.

I turn to Levi. "So, do you still love me?"

"I told you I would. No matter what."

We both look at each other, and I can't help but giggle. I know today was a lot for Levi. He's trying to be supportive, but I can see he's holding back what he wants to say.

"Okay, I was not expecting what I saw today."

We both laugh this time.

"I knew it."

During the next three years, my siblings and I continue to make occasional trips to Stratford to see Mom. Not much has changed in her life, other than having to pay an additional fifty dollars every month to cover the damages she caused from the fire.

CHAPTER TWENTY-ONE

Engagement

2008–2010

I graduate with honors from a personal support worker night school program in 2008 and find work during the day at a nonprofit organization that supports adults who are developmentally delayed and have mental illnesses, brain injuries, and dual diagnoses. The manager in charge of hiring has the clients from the group home interview me, which is a big decision for them and empowers them to advocate for themselves.

My position originally starts as a nighttime monitor from 11:00 p.m. to 8:00 a.m. I live rent-free in the basement of the clients' house and make sure they stay safe during the night. In the mornings, I prepare breakfast for them, give them their meds, prepare their lunch, help them get dressed for the day, and walk them to their day program.

The job sounds easy and simple. They fail to tell me about the woman named Kaytie, who doesn't sleep. She constantly sneaks into the kitchen and eats whole loaves of frozen bread, and anything else she can find. She takes toilet paper from the bathroom to make spitballs and shoots them around her room with a straw. I run up the stairs every time I hear her spit through the baby monitor I keep beside my bed. Eventually I give up asking her to stop and get used to the spitting sound. Every morning, her room looks as if it snowed overnight. In the mornings, I simply wake her up, say good morning, and remind her that the broom and dustpan are by her door. She knows to clean up after herself.

I love these ladies so much and have many wonderful and funny stories from supporting them.

One spring day, I take the three housemates I support, Kaytie, Renée, and Kelly, to Springbank Park in London. We pack a picnic and spend the afternoon down by the water. Kelly, my short and stout friend with Down syndrome, notices a goose walking behind her in the park. She starts walking a little faster. So does the goose. She quickly waddles from side to side, pumping her arms. Fear grows in her eyes as she bounces forward. She turns around to see the goose, nose down, streamlining toward her, and screams my name, "Wainie! Wainie!" Both the goose and my friend's waddle turn into sprinting. I laugh hysterically while chasing the goose that's chasing Kelly. "Run, Kelly! Faster!" is all I can yell.

"Goose. Got me good. Bite my wegs! Kick him in da neck. Hate ducks."

I also work multiple jobs within their organization, including the day program, many group homes, and a restaurant called the Mercantile, where I supervise and support clients as they prepare and serve food; wash, dry, and put away dishes; and expand their social skills with their community. It's one of my favorite jobs. Most individuals I support radiate joy and love, and are among the most amazing, forgiving, and accepting people I know. I wholeheartedly look forward to seeing their faces at work and strive to mirror their qualities.

The restaurant bustles with customers who are enthusiastic and supportive of our staff and their desire to work. Our clients enjoy playful conversations with their customers over coffee and banter back and forth about their rival sports teams and the weather. It is soul-filling to witness such pure interactions between people without any judgment, but just acceptance, patience, and love.

During the evenings, I support men and women in their group homes. I help with their daily needs, such as bathing, meal preparation, administration of medications, grocery shopping, budgeting, tracking their spending, and taking them to activities within the community. My favorite is karaoke night on Wednesdays.

Many times, I work twenty-four hours a day. I start the day with an 8:00 a.m. to 4:00 p.m. shift at the day program, then work a 4:00 p.m. to 11:00 p.m. shift in one of the group homes, and finally work the 11:00 p.m. to 8:00 a.m. shift as the overnight monitor.

One night, at the end of my shift at the Mercantile, my phone rings. I know it's Levi and get excited. We're supposed to go look at engagement rings tonight after work.

"Hey babe!" I say, grinning from ear to ear. "Are you almost here? I'm just about done closing the store."

"Honey, you're not going to like this. My brother needs to borrow my truck tonight, so I can't come to pick you up. The mall closes at nine anyway. Let's go another day when we have more time."

I'm disappointed, to say the least. "What? Levi, no! We still have time to get to the mall if I race out of here now."

"Just drive here to Mom and Dad's after your shift tonight. We'll hang out," he promises.

I insist we still have time to make it to the mall before closing. "I'll pick you up. We'll race to the mall. I want to look at the rings, even if it's just for a few minutes."

"Okay. Your choice."

Once I close the restaurant for the night, I speed to Levi's parents' house. I impatiently wait in his laneway, which is usually full of vehicles. I honk the horn, but he doesn't come out. *You should have been ready, Levi!* I'm frustrated. I get out of the car with a furrowed brow and march across the deck to the sunroom.

No way...

I open the door and immediately notice several candles lit on a small round table covered in red linens. *What is going on?* Orange flames dance across the darkened sunroom's walls. I read three separate photo frames: "I. Love. You." There are roses on a silver platter, and their petals are scattered across the table and floor. I pick up the open note on the table, which simply reads, "Do you remember where we first met? If so, meet me there." I take a moment to gather my thoughts. *Could this be the night I get engaged?* I open the door to the house and scream hello, but all the lights are off.

I blow out all the candles and race out the front door. My car burns rubber in reverse out of their long laneway, and I begin to drive down the road to Hanna and Gus's place, forgetting they moved and don't live there anymore. I pull over to the side of the road and wonder whether I should trespass onto a stranger's property. I take the chance.

God's hand-painted cotton-candy sky has gifted the evening with the perfect amount of ambiance. The sun is setting and reflecting itself off the sparkling pond's water, and the whispers through the trees are calling me toward the pond's island. Levi and I have so many memories here. It's where he taught me how to fish and how to start a fire by strategically placing sticks in a tepee shape while insisting it's a beneficial skill I should know. It's the place he held me close when I tossed pictures, letters, and poems from my previous life into the burning flames of the fire. It's where I promised him my future. It's the place we sat bundled up together while deep in conversation after a late-night skate on a cold winter's night, talking about life and our future together. Healing happened on this island. It's my safe place with Levi.

I see Levi standing beneath the tree's canopy, holding twenty-four long-stemmed red roses. He looks so handsome. This is the moment I've been waiting for my whole life. Tears well up in my eyes as I approach him.

"Honey," I begin. "I smell like french fries and—"

"Shh … It's okay," he laughs. "Let me start. From the moment I met you, I knew you were special—unlike anyone I had ever met. You have been so patient in waiting for this to happen. Truth is, I've had this ring for a while but was waiting for the right moment. I've always known it was you, Lainie. We've been through so much together, but it's all led us to this very moment. I'm proud of how far you've come in your life. Your strength continues to amaze me. I want you to be my life partner, the mother of my children, the one I grow old and gray with. With that being said"—he drops down to one knee and opens the ring box—"I was wondering if you'd make me the happiest man in the world. Lainie, will you marry me?"

I gasp at the beauty of the custom-designed white gold ring with a raised round brilliant cut diamond in the center and four smaller diamonds on either side. I wipe my eyes with shaking hands and shout yes. I stare at the shining diamond ring as Levi slides it up my left ring finger. "Levi. It's so beautiful." I lean into him and pull him close. "I can't wait to live life together with you." I am elated about being engaged and can hardly wait to tell his parents.

I feel so many emotions. I am overjoyed, of course. I feel the belonging and acceptance I've been craving my whole life. I feel the promise of unconditional love. I feel as though I've found my safe place with Levi. I also feel an emptiness, as if something is missing. I toss the feeling to the side and carry on in my joy.

I follow Levi to his parents' house and excitedly tell his family about our engagement. Maggie cheers, throws her hands up, and wraps me in a hug. "We were downstairs hiding the whole time you were here!"

"You were? There weren't any cars in the laneway."

"We parked all the vehicles behind the shop. I can't believe you blew out all the candles before you left!"

"I didn't want to start a fire," I laugh.

Levi's brother shouts, "Congratulations, sis!" and embraces me with me hug. "Pretty sure you left tire marks in the laneway from speeding out of here."

"Sorry," I laugh again.

"Congratulations, lovebirds!" Manuel shouts in his Portuguese accent, pumping his hands up and down and dancing toward us in excitement. He always makes me laugh.

We call Levi's *Oma* and his Portuguese grandparents and my sisters on FaceTime, who are all so happy for us. I am ecstatic too, but the realization that I don't have parents to call makes me feel sad. I tell Levi I need a few minutes alone to text some friends. I close the door of the bedroom behind me and sit on the bed. I want to call my mom to tell her about our engagement, but she lives far away and doesn't own a phone. I can't call my dad, because I've never met him and know nothing about him. I can't call my foster parents from my childhood, because I don't know their information or how to find them. I want to call Lisa, but I've severed the relationship with her.

Levi's family loves me well. Why isn't that enough for me?

They celebrate my accomplishments. They spoil me. They love me unconditionally. Still, there is a gaping void I feel from being a parentless child born into a dysfunctional and chaotic family. I know that no one other than my biological parents can fill the emptiness I feel. The painful acceptance of my loss hurts. I'm chasing a dream that will never be my reality.

I have impossible dreams of my future with my mother. I'm devastated that I can't make her better—for herself or for me. She'll never be able to drive to my house to visit me. She'll never pop over with bridal magazines or snuggle up on the couch with me while we excitedly flip through wedding pages. She can't help me try on wedding dresses or plan my bridal shower. She won't be sitting in the front row in a red dress at my wedding or giving a heartfelt speech at the reception. She won't be holding my hand during childbirth or babysitting her grandkids. None of these dreams will come true, and the realization of it overwhelms me.

My fairytale dream of having my biological father walk me down the aisle is a dead wish that will never be granted. He's missed everything in my life, including walking me down the aisle on my wedding day. I sink into a moment of despair. My anxious thoughts come flooding back. I don't feel that I'm enough—for myself or for Levi. I worry I'll fail in marriage or that Levi will stop loving me when things get hard. I wonder if I'm equipped to "do forever" with someone. I consider whether it's better to avoid marriage than to be brave and choose love. I worry Levi won't enjoy living with me when we move in together after our wedding day. I wipe my eyes and beg myself to pull it together. I take a deep breath and practice my smile when I open the door. When I do, I am greeted with hugs and welcomed with celebration.

This should be enough for me.

CHAPTER TWENTY-TWO

I Do

2010–2012

The wedding day finally arrives. There are 215 guests in attendance, and I feel like Cinderella at the royal ball. The bridesmaids and I get ready at Levi's parents' place, and the men get ready at the house Levi and I have recently purchased together. We'll finally be living together after the honeymoon, and I can't wait.

Long dark brown curls dangle down my back. An embedded Swarovski crystal loop hangs from my necklace, and two matching earrings complete the set. They're a gift to me from the Porters. Since our wedding theme is mostly black and white, I decide to add a black sash around my waist with a sparkling crystal brooch. My makeup is professionally done, and the photographer we hire is fantastic. We're proud to not have any debt from the wedding or from the down payment on our first home.

When everyone is seated and quiet, the gifted pianist begins to play. Each note dances and echoes within the walls of the auditorium. My bridesmaids—Rachel, Ellie, Rosie, Maria, and my best friend, Amy—make their way down the aisle one by one to meet their groomsmen. When they've all found their places, the pianist gradually works her way into playing the entrance song. I walk to the double doors and wait for my cue to begin my walk. I look into the loving eyes of the standing men and women who have chosen to celebrate with us—those who are related to me and have loved me for years and those who have chosen to love me on their own.

Mom has refused to be a part of my wedding day and has chosen not to come. Standing alone without my father beside me stings for a moment, but I know God is right here by my side. I'm proud of myself, and I know God is proud of me too. I breathe deeply through my nose and fill my chest to hold back tears and to calm myself. Then I pray.

God, you are a good father. You have pursued me, fought for me, and showed me a life-saving love that I hold so close. Thank you for this day and for blessing me with Levi, whose only desire is to reflect you. Thank you for always being by my side, especially at this very moment. Walk with me now, Jesus, and all the days of my life.

I look to Levi, my beaming husband, and smile the biggest smile. I hear the music get louder and stronger, which is the pianist's way of letting me know it's time to walk. Levi's eyes are reeling me toward him. I want to run into his arms, but I don't. Instead, I walk slowly without breaking eye contact once. He makes his way toward me and meets me halfway up the aisle. He reaches for my hand and pulls me into a tight embrace. He whispers to me how beautiful I look, then awkwardly asks whether he's allowed to kiss me. I tell him not yet, and we both laugh. He releases me, gives my hand three squeezes, and walks with me to the altar.

The congregation sings a couple hymns together, and a special song is performed by Rosie and our friend Finn, called "When God Made You," by Newsong. The pastor announces that it's time for Levi to recite his vows to me. Levi's crimson cheeks and nervous mannerisms make me smile. I am attracted to every part of him. Levi, who's memorized his vows, looks into my eyes and anxiously begins speaking.

"Lainie, I love you. Today we're getting married because of our love for each other. I want to spend the rest of our lives together. I'm going to love you until the day I die. In sickness and in health, in the ups and the downs. No matter what God puts in front of us, I promise to be by your side. I promise to love you, putting your own needs before my own and owning up to any mistakes I'll make along the way. I promise to put God at the center of our relationship and to look to him for answers and trust him on this journey he has for us. Lainie, I just want to take care of you, provide for you, and be your best friend. I want to give you my all and help you be the best you possibly can. Lainie, I love you today, I love you tomorrow and forever."

My heart melts when Levi looks into my eyes and tells me he just wants to provide and take care of me. His words are salve to my soul, and I know he means them. There is an auditorium full of people, but it feels as though Levi and I are the only ones in the room. It's my turn to recite the vows I've written for Levi.

"Levi, I have been praying for you since I was a little girl. Late at night, I'd lie in bed and pray for you, my future husband. I prayed that wherever you were in this world, God would keep you safe and protect you, that he would watch over you until we could be together. And here we are today. I continue to pray for you and constantly thank God for answering a little girl's prayer. I knew I wanted to marry you when I experienced the way you treated me so differently from anyone I've ever known. I hadn't known what it was like to be wholly loved by someone, to be treated properly, and you've shown me that. You've shown me that I do deserve to be loved, that I do have worth, and that I'll always be good enough. I'll never be able to tell you how much that means to me. I finally know what true love is, and I never want to be without it. I'm so excited to marry you today, to finally be able to fall asleep with you every night …"

Here Levi looks at the crowd, raises his eyebrows multiple times and grins from ear to ear. The audience laughs, and Levi shrugs his shoulders as if to say, "Well, it's true."

"… and one day have a family of our own and show them the same love that you've shown me. I'm excited to grow old with you, even when the wrinkles start to form on our faces and our hair starts turning gray. I promise to encourage you, inspire you, and make you laugh. I promise to comfort you in times of sorrow and love you in good times and bad; when life seems easy, and when it seems really hard; when our love is simple, and when it takes constant effort. I want you to know I'll be there through it all. Levi, I promise to love you, to be your best friend, to respect you and support you, to be patient, and to always work as a team. I want you to know you'll always be my top priority. I love you."

Our pastor pronounces us husband and wife, and Levi and I share our first kiss as a married couple. Our family and friends cheer and stand to their feet as we exit down the aisle hand in hand and smiling from ear to ear. The reception is an absolute blast. Dinner is mouthwatering, the speeches are hilarious and touching and the music has us dancing all night long. It is the most magical day of my life. I am surrounded with love the entire day. I finally feel I belong. I feel loved completely. I feel everything I longed for in my childhood.

We have our bags packed and ready for our flight to British Columbia, Canada, early tomorrow morning. We get off the plane and breathe in the fresh, clean mountain air. Our hotel room, at the base of the mountain, is dreamy and romantic. On the table is a bottle of champagne, chocolate-dipped strawberries, and a lovely card from our family back home telling us our honeymoon has been paid for. The next evening, Levi and I board the gondola and enjoy a slow ride to the top. I nestle myself into Levi's arms and point out the mountain bikers, black bears with their cubs, and skiers wiping out in the snow.

We reach the summit of Blackcomb Mountain and witness one of the most romantic sunsets we've ever seen. We are totally in awe of God's breathtaking creation and full of gratitude for our journey. We take a few moments to reflect upon all we've accomplished and prepare our hearts for our next adventure as a married couple.

We enjoy an incredible week of romance, dining out, swimming, touring, and lounging. Levi has signed himself up for an exhilarating bungee experience in Whistler and encourages me to do it with him. Now I feel fearless and pay a large sum to jump too. We're led to a tiny metal bridge, where we wait to jump with tied feet and open arms, 160 feet above the glacier-fed Cheakamus River. I can barely even stand on the bridge. I'm clinging to the sides with my eyes closed. I know for sure that I'll be forfeiting my turn. No amount of money I pay will ever make me do something so irresponsible. Levi is nervous too but full of adrenaline. He flies outward and flings around like a bobble-head toy. He gets reeled up by his feet to the bridge we're standing on, red-faced and smiling. Instead of taking Levi's gear off, they ask him whether he wants to take my turn and jump again.

"Honey, come on. You can do this, babe," Levi pleads.

"I'm not dying today. No way. No how. No chance."

Without hesitation, Levi takes his second jump and plummets down toward the rock-filled river between mountain cliffs and forest. We both get T-shirts that read, "I bungee jumped in Whistler, B.C." The shirt of shame—I never wear it.

When our romantic week in beautiful British Columbia comes to an end, I'm sad to leave. But I also can't wait to walk through the front doors of our small, renovated home with Levi. It's time to leave and begin our lives together back home.

CHAPTER TWENTY-THREE

Mom Finally Gets Help

2011

Rachel and I make a trip to Stratford and notice that Mom's health and living conditions are worse than ever. Mom is urinating blood and complaining of stomach pain. Rachel and I leave Mom's apartment and go downstairs to exit the building to breathe. We call our siblings and ask them to come to Stratford to see Mom so we can discuss our options together. Rachel and I are crying in her van. Mom needs help right away. She could die if we leave her like this.

Rachel is a genius when it comes to connecting with resources within the government and the community. She knows the system inside and out. Rachel begins to research and work out a plan. We head to the courthouse to see whether we can speak to a judge. We know it's almost impossible, considering we don't have an open case, or a highly paid lawyer to represent us, but we have love and panic in our hearts for our mother, and we know the risk of trying is worth it. The receptionist says the judge doesn't have time to see us, especially without representation, but we've inherited Mom's stubborn gene. We wait. We plead. We refuse to leave. Rachel tells the woman we need to see the judge today because it's a matter of life or death for our mother.

The receptionist senses our pain and urgency. She clears her throat. "I'll see what I can do. Wait here, please." She gets up and leaves her desk. After waiting a while, she returns. "Today is your lucky day. This rarely happens, but the judge has decided to meet with you." We are thrilled. Rachel enters the courtroom, and I follow close behind her. She stands confidently before the judge and fights for our mother. I sit behind her in the courtroom, in awe of her professionalism. I don't know what she's saying. I just think, *Yep! That's right! Exactly! Nailed it!* Rachel knows what she needs to say to get the judge's help. She advocates for our mother and explains her living conditions. The judge listens to her carefully and orders Mom to be immediately evaluated by psychiatric professionals at the hospital. I am so proud of my big sister. She's fighting for the woman who traumatized her childhood. It's a huge display of love, loyalty, leadership, forgiveness, and grace.

The judge sends two police officers to Mom's apartment right away to escort her to the local psychiatric ward for assessment. I know this isn't going to be easy. I'm conflicted, with warring emotions, as we follow the officers back to Mom's place. I feel pumped and energized about Rachel performing a miracle with the judge. I feel relieved Mom won't be returning to her apartment. I also feel an immense amount of guilt and betrayal. Surprising Mom with another trip back to the Psychiatric Ward all these years later isn't going to be pleasant.

Mom sees the officers in the doorway of the building. She turns directly toward them.

"Are you looking for me?"

"No, ma'am," they kindly respond.

Shoot!

Trying not to worry Mom, while also letting the police know they'd just walked past the woman they'd come here for, is tricky. When Mom looks away, we wave our hands like mimes and use facial expressions to get the officers' attention. *They're going to think we're the ones who need help.* The officers finally get the hint.

"Are you Annie?" one of the officers asks Mom.

When she answers yes, my heart fills with guilt and betrayal and sinks to the bottom of my chest. Fear darts from Mom's eyes to ours like lasers.

"Did you do this? Did you call them on me? Why would you do this to me?!"

Adrenaline bubbles under my skin and makes my body shiver.

We assure Mom of her safety and remind her she's not in any trouble. "Mom, you're okay." Rachel says. "You're only going for a car ride to the hospital to make sure you're okay. We promise we'll be right behind you in the van, and with you the whole time." Before the police officer lowers her head into the car, we tell her we love her and that we'll see her soon.

The sterile, chemical smell upon entering the hospital is strong enough to singe nostril hair. The walls are an off-white creamy color that has been thickly sprayed over concrete blocks. Not a single piece of artwork hangs on the wall. I suppose artwork can be upsetting to someone struggling with mental health, depending on how the person interprets it.

We stay in the psychiatric wing of the hospital with Mom for hours, answering questions, filling out paperwork, and waiting for the staff. Ellie arrives at the hospital and joins us in the waiting room. The ringing alarms and beepers are a continual background noise, but the patients in line at the nurses' station, who continue to ask questions they've been given answers to already, don't seem to mind the noise.

"Compared to the way you're living now, Mom, this will feel like a hotel," I start.

"I like my place," Mom says. "I don't want to stay here."

"It's only temporary. They have a TV you can watch anytime in the common area over there." I point to the area with six anchored-to-the-floor chairs facing the TV. "I bet it has more than three channels, Mom. Just look how big and beautiful it is. It's so fancy it even has a remote, so you don't have to get up and click a knob anymore."

"Oh, really?" Mom says, raising her black penciled-in eyebrows. "That's nice." She really does think it's nice. She turns to look toward the common area with a grin on her face, but it quickly disappears after she notices a man sitting in one of the chairs. "I don't want to sit with any of those delusional people. I don't know them. I like watching the news, anyway. They probably like other shows."

"If they try to steal the remote from you, just stand up, scream really loud, and wave your arms like you're delusional too. They'll leave you alone. It works for me every time."

Mom laughs.

"They'll help you with your laundry. You won't have to use your bathtub anymore. You can take a nice, hot shower without stinking clothes beneath your feet."

Mom raises her eyebrows again. "Really? I don't like going downstairs in my apartment to do laundry. There are insane people down there."

"You're safe here, Mom." I promise her. "You don't have to worry. The workers here are paid big bucks to always keep you safe. You'll have your own room—one you don't have to give to your cat. I still can't believe you let the cat have your bedroom."

"The cat really liked that room," Mom insists. "It was okay for me to sleep on the couch."

I laugh. "You should have seen that cat run when we opened the door, Mom. It looked possessed."

"Yeah, the humane society took him after the fire. Did you know that? I went and picked him up right away and brought him back home with me, but he started acting insane and getting nasty, so I brought him back to the humane society for good."

"He'll have a better life there, Mom," Ellie says bluntly.

"Yeah, I was sad about it though."

"I'm sure you were," agrees Ellie. "He was your only companion."

Rachel is looking over the paperwork. "You'll be eating well here, Mom. The chefs downstairs in the kitchen will prepare you three well-balanced meals every day that consist of more than just potatoes and pasta. The best part is you don't have to cook a single one of them. They'll take care of all of that for you. Meals are served at the same time every day too, so you won't have to worry about going hungry or when you're going to eat next."

The best part of this whole psych ward situation is Mom finally being medicated. Our hearts are brimming with hope that Mom will experience a quality of life and have freedom over her restless mind.

I can see the relief in Mom's eyes about having three meals a day and not worrying about missing meals. The gentleman who is watching TV gets up from his seat and displays the majority of his plumber's crack to the rest of the residents. He stretches, prolonging the view, then turns in our direction and smiles at Mom. Mom is disgusted, and her expression makes us all laugh hysterically. Her face always tells exactly how she's feeling.

Ellie is nearly out of breath from laughing. "Who knows, Mom? Maybe you'll fall in love here. That might be your future husband right there."

"Why would you say something like that, Ellie?" Mom scoffs. "That guy's a bum."

"A large part of him is, yes," Ellie laughs. "I'm just joking, Mom."

"Okay, good. I'm not interested in men anymore anyway," Mom says.

The unison of our laughter is contagious and lifts our souls.

Lonnie Junior and Blaire arrive to support Mom, and the five of us are led to a small family meeting room. It's good to see them. The stained red rolling chairs surrounding the large rectangular meeting table bring an odd sense of peace to my weary soul. There are other struggling families like ours who have sat here trying to make sense of their lives too.

Mom has nine very different children who are all resilient, strong-headed, and opinionated. But it doesn't matter today. Today is about our mother. We continue to fill the time by telling stories of our childhood and the wild things we did and saw. We're happy to be together, even if it is in the psych ward. Mom is not alone. I watch her look around the room and admire her grown children she forfeited. Our love for her unifies us and gives us common ground. We don't know what Mom's future holds, but at this moment she's safe, and that's all we want.

It's time for Mom to be admitted. The mood in the room immediately changes. It's time to say good-bye to Mom. The nurse walks Mom through the heavy glass doors that separate us. My heart is pulling to keep her close to me. Mom turns her head to look at her children and says, "I love you." I see my mother in that moment—my beautiful, neglected, abandoned, mistreated mother, alone in the psych ward. Mom offers a half-smile, lifts her pale hand, and waves a gentle good-bye. There is fear and pain in her eyes. It pierces my heart and destroys me emotionally. I'm trying to understand why this separation hurts so much, and then the memory overtakes me. Her fearful expression mirrored the same one I gave her from the back of the Thompsons' car window many years ago, on the day I was peeled from her leg and forced into a car, never to live with her again.

We hope the hospital psychiatrists deem Mom incapable of taking care of herself so we can get her proper support and assistance, but because Mom hasn't had two hospital admissions in five years, she doesn't qualify for a community treatment order. However, because there is toxic mold in Mom's apartment, it qualifies her for a thirty-day hospital admission.

After thirty days with Mom, the psychiatrist has sufficient evidence to prove she is incapable of taking care of herself. Mom is released from the psychiatric ward and sent to a halfway house with support workers in and out of the home.

A few weeks later, Rachel invites me to lunch and says she wants to talk to me about something *immediately.*

After getting seated and ordering drinks, I beg her to tell me what's going on.

"Remember that awful gut feeling you had about Mom the day you drove to Stratford?"

"Yeah ... Why?"

"I had the same feeling this week. I just knew something was wrong, so I drove there too."

"Whoa. It's crazy how connected we are."

"I know; I thought the same thing."

"Is Mom okay? What did you find?"

"So, I go to Mom's halfway house and bang on the door. Eventually, after what feels like forever, a resident finally lets me in. I realize there's no staff in the house. I go to Mom's room, and she's lying in bed, barely responsive, totally dehydrated, and can barely move."

"But she was just in the hospital. They didn't notice she was sick?" I ask, confused.

"I know. The hospital unknowingly released Mom with an infection. She stopped eating and drinking. She just kept mumbling about how she wanted to go home, back to her condemned apartment."

"What did you do?"

"I called Mom an ambulance and had her readmitted to the hospital."

"Where was the infection?"

"In her bladder again."

"Okay, so she's back at the home they had her in?"

"No, Mom won't go back there. They suggested sending her to a shared-housing home for mental health patients, but Mom won't go there either."

"Well, there aren't any other options right now."

Rachel laughs nervously in a way I recognize. I can see in her eyes she's in shock and needs to tell me more.

"Oh, no. What? Why are you laughing like that?"

"The hospital psychiatrist talked to me about Mom's lack of options and suggested she come live with me."

I lift my eyebrows and stare blankly into Rachel's eyes, my response hanging in the air between us. Eventually I shake my head in disbelief and blurt out the only thing I can think of.

"Are you joking?"

Rachel laughs nervously again. "I know. The psychiatrist's recommendation definitely caught me off guard."

"So you're going to?"

"I was cautious and hesitant about the decision, but I've considered it carefully. We'll take Mom in until she can find temporary housing."

CHAPTER TWENTY-FOUR

Becoming a Mother

2012–2015

Levi and I want to start a family. I don't want to work the evening and weekend shifts forever. I want to be home eating dinner with my family every night. The school board has the best hours, which include every summer off, and weekends and all holidays too; it sounds like a dream. I love my current job of supporting adults and want to continue working with them, but I also want to get hired by the school board and support children from kindergarten through high school with complex needs.

I know, for myself, that if I don't go to college before having children, I won't go at all. The organization I work for has recently mandated staff to have their developmental service worker diploma, so I figure it's the perfect time to enroll myself in the two-year DSW college program. I want to learn more about mental illnesses, developmental disabilities, early childhood development, and the effects trauma has on the brain. I want to understand my mother's paranoid schizophrenia and learn how the brain works. Maybe it'll help soften my heart toward her.

In 2012, during the second year of my studies, I find out I'm pregnant. I jump from the toilet and trip over the pants still around my ankles. I gather myself and yell for Levi to get in the bathroom, "We're having a baby!" I exclaim. We are overjoyed and filled with excitement. I can't wait to tell his parents and my family. I can't keep a secret to save my life, so I waste no time getting into the car to drive around the country block to tell them.

I naively believe motherhood will heal the childhood pain I've suppressed. I hope the love I feel for my husband, Levi, will blossom and our family will be happy. I can hardly wait. I fight sickness, constant nausea, body aches, and tiredness while attending school full-time and working evenings. I graduate college with honors and attend the graduation ceremony while eight months pregnant. I am twenty-seven years old, and Levi twenty-six, when we become first-time parents to our beautiful blonde, blue-eyed baby girl Violet. Twelve short months later, in 2014, we become parents again to a brown-eyed brunette named Olivia. Our girls' births are the greatest moments of our lives.

I would have given my life for my girls the moment they exited my body and looked into my eyes. They depend on me for everything. This is my chance to undo all my mother's mistakes. I swear to be the best mom, to embrace their every need with affection, to daily bathe them in my love, to correct their behavior with patience and understanding, and to always be gentle.

I have no idea what is to come.

I'm like a runner at the start of a race, full of adrenaline with my knees bent, backside in the air, and my hands placed shoulder width apart on the black tar. I'm ready to begin my sprint into motherhood. I focus my eyes straight ahead, grind my teeth into my mouthguard, and prepare myself for the takeoff. But when the man with the gun puts his hand in the air and pulls the trigger, I fall flat on my face, skin my knees, and cover my ears. The trigger. I forgot about the trigger.

My girls are not even one and two yet, and my deepest, darkest fears rip through my mind, replaying flashbacks of childhood trauma. Memories of abuse and neglect send flaming daggers straight through my heart. The joy I feel as a new mother pours out from my scarred chest. I can't stop looking at my innocent little girls and seeing myself at their age. I miss my husband and need him.

Levi's a talented landscaper who specializes in natural stonework. He, his boss, and his coworker have accepted a unique job opportunity for a very successful, well-known man on his personal property. While the pay raise will be good for our little family, it comes with a heavy cost; the job will last over three years, and as it's a few hours from home, Levi will live with the team during the week.

I feel isolated living in the middle of nowhere in a fixer-upper house with our two toddlers while he's away at work. Every night, I wake alone to the same nightmare, struggling to breathe. I experience tormenting visions of men, like a pack of wolves, surrounding my girls. I am full of fear as I gruesomely kill men who lunge toward my children. Every night is a panicked rush to escape locked rooms and dark alleys while I try to keep my girls upright and quiet while I run. I can't trust anyone in my dreams. They capture my crying, terrified girls and pull them just out of my reach. I stretch my arms in agony toward my daughters' fingertips but can't grip their hands.

I wake to the sound of my own scream. My heart is racing, I am short of breath, and my rib cage hurts. My throat is constricted, I am sweating, and I begin to cry hysterically. I push the covers off and walk next door to the girls' room to see them sleeping peacefully in their beds. I can't keep living like this. I lean my back against the hallway wall and take the only support it has to offer. I look to the ceiling, the place my prayers seem to be bouncing off of lately. With tears pouring down my face in utter defeat, I slide down the wall to the floor. *God, where are you? This is torture.*

What's wrong with me? Anxiety eats me alive. Fear controls my every move. I am always overwhelmed. My mind exhausts my body. I feel as if I'm in a crossfire of spiritual warfare. *God, save me.*

I should be happy, but I'm struggling and don't understand why. I'm a new mother. This should be a joyful time. I feel guilty for the feelings and thoughts I'm having and try to convince myself that I'm just overtired. I blame it on the hormones. I blame other people. I try to pray it away. I push my childhood pain deep within myself, much like loading an explosive shell into a cannon. Becoming a mother, especially to two little girls so close together, lights the cannon's fuse and explodes every shard of brokenness I've ever carried into the world for all to see. It's loud. Everyone hears it, everyone sees it, and many people I love are hurt by it. I feel naked in a crowd. I'm humiliated.

Having two babies in twelve months delivers an afterbirth of postpartum depression. My family doctor gives me the diagnosis, but I believe I'm also struggling with complex post-traumatic stress disorder, among other things. I've never seen a psychologist or paid a therapist or counselor outside of the church, so I don't tell anyone my self-diagnosis. My kinship home raised me to believe that God is the ultimate healer and counselor, and that I don't need therapy outside of the church or medication that alters my mind. My relationship with Levi and others I love are suffering, my mental health is declining, and my babies aren't getting the best version of their mother. I am irritable, depressed, and lonely. I don't want to become reliant on medication for the rest of my life, but I'm willing to take it for as long as I need to. My healing journey needs to begin within my heart, and I need to be in a good headspace to do that.

I need to revisit the pain of my childhood so I can heal my inner child and move forward with peace in my life. I crave peace and want to know what it feels like both in my body and in my mind. I know the self-inflicted incisions of digging into my past will cause me pain. I don't want to revisit the life I have tried so hard to hide, but I know it's necessary.

CHAPTER TWENTY-FIVE

Generational Trauma

2018

Mom is at our house for a sleepover. She loves being here with our family, and we enjoy having her here. After getting the kids to sleep, Levi retreats to our bedroom to give me and Mom some privacy to talk. Steam shoots from the boiling kettle and screams at me to jump from the kitchen chair to turn it off. I invite Mom to the table where the tea fixings and snacks are set up. I fill our mugs with boiled water and place Mom's in front of her. As she drops her tea bag into her cup, I tell her I have hard questions to ask—questions I've been wanting answers to since childhood. I'm a thirty-two-year-old woman who can finally talk rationally with my mother in conversation. It feels like a long-awaited miracle. Mom is medicated and stable now. She spent her whole life, up until her late fifties, imprisoned in her own mind without relief. She's a meek, mild, and tender soul now, much different from who she used to be. I don't worry as much anymore about her shutting down, having manic episodes, or throwing egregious accusations at me when we're together.

I want to talk with her about my absent father and hear the hard details about my childhood. I would like to learn about her life too. Mom reluctantly agrees but tells me she doesn't like talking about him or our past.

"Your father, Marco, was addicted to cocaine, hash, and marijuana and he loved alcohol, too."

Mom pauses and readjusts herself in my tall-backed

leather kitchen chair. Talking about him is already making her uncomfortable. I feel partly selfish for pushing her in conversation; however, I need to make sense of my life and feel I deserve some explanations. I need to hear what happened in her own words.

Mom sighs and looks around the room for a minute, unable to focus on anything. Her overly bleached blonde hair doesn't move when she turns her head. Her green eyes finally meet mine, and she half-smiles. I reach across the table to hold her soft hand. "Anyway," she begins again, "he's from a big Italian family and is one of fourteen kids. All the boys' names started with the letter M. Isn't that something?" she asks. "He was only five two. He was just little," she says with a laugh.

I imagine my five-foot two father walking the streets, puffing his chest out like a bulldog, and walking like a rooster beside my slender five-foot-ten mother.

I don't have a single memory of my father. He abused my mom and abandoned his kids. That's all the information I need. I was twenty-seven years old when I saw a picture of his face for the first time. My eldest sister, Colleen, found his Facebook profile and sent it to me. She knew without a doubt the man in the photo was my father. The single picture was taken decades ago, and there was no information written about him. I absorbed every bit of detail and tried to match his face with the stories I'd heard about him. I investigated his features and looked for shadows of them in my face. The resemblance was astounding. I chuckled to myself because he looked like Super Mario from Nintendo. I imagined my father flicking his bushy eyebrows up and down at Mom while raising his right arm and shouting, "It's a-me, a-Mar-i-o!" He had a small, thin face; a big nose; a thick black mustache; small brown eyes, and a red-and-white hat on. Mom was twenty-five, and Marco was still a teenager when they met. "He always fibbed about his age. I never knew how old he actually was."

How could you not know? I think to myself. "Did you ever try to leave?"

"I tried to move away from him once, but he showed up unexpectedly when we were leaving. He helped load our furniture, then hopped into the front seat with the moving man and hitched a ride to find out where we were going. He was out of his mind."

The thought of my dad jumping into the moving van while Mom was trying to leave him makes me laugh. He was a leech sucking the life from Mom, who was numb to the feeling of being drained.

I felt the sting of my father's absence growing up. When I saw little girls laughing with their daddies or riding on their strong shoulders, I'd smile because I genuinely felt their joy. But like a weed, sadness always came, sprouting its ugly head, overtaking the moment, and reminding me of what I didn't have.

Father. I'm still not sure what to call him.

"Do you think he ever loved me?"

"I think so," she replies.

I think so.

I pause on that. *Pause. Pause. Pause. Breathe. Okay … that really hurts. More than I thought it would, actually.* I breathe deep through my nose and exhale. *He chose not to love me.* Truth spills into my heart like alcohol over an open wound. I need to remove the infection of false realities I created to avoid feeling rejection and abandonment. I need to obliterate who I created him to be and release the dream of him being a changed man who's been looking for me my whole life, and the idea that he'll apologize and want a relationship. Letting go of this dream is harder than I imagined. The dam I store my tears behind is about to give way. *Dismiss your feelings, Lainie. Now's not the time.* I relinquish the brewing hurricane of uneasiness stirring within me to make Mom more comfortable. I do that. I hold my breath beneath thrashing tides while lifting her to the surface for air. I sacrifice my authenticity in exchange with her feeling safe with me. Mom doesn't trust anyone anymore, and I want to be that person for her—even if she wasn't safe for me.

With glassy eyes, I ask Mom, "How did you meet him?" I bat my teary eyelashes to lighten both our moods. I know whatever details come next will be anything but cute or flirtatious. "Is it as romantic as I think it's going to be?"

Mom takes a sip of her tea. Her plum lipstick smears all around the rim of my white mug. She scoffs at her own disturbing thoughts then shares a story so shocking that my breath catches in my throat.

"That was the first time you met my father?" I ask. "With him barging through your door and dominating your body? I knew it was bad, but not to that extent, Mom." I shake my head in disbelief and take another sip of tea.

"His brother Matteo did it to me first. He must have went home and told Marco about me. I didn't know he was psychotic then."

"How did you not know? Him taking advantage of you wasn't your first clue? What did you do? You just let him stay?"

"I took him out to a restaurant and bought him a nice steak dinner."

"What?" I ask. "You're telling me you bought the breaking-and-entering man a steak instead of judo-chopping him in the neck? Did you keep your steak knife in your pocket after dinner?"

"No," she laughs. "I liked to spoil him sometimes."

I loathe the men who hurt my mother; I do. I feel terrible for the way men treated her. Witnessing that level of abuse as a child was horrific. Mom chose men over my safety, and her needs over mine. The reality of that statement is heartbreaking. We children were starving at home. We had no money for groceries, yet Mom bought steak dinners for herself and Marco to enjoy. No wonder he stuck around.

I question her. "What was it about him that made you want to stay with him?"

"He would never go away. He followed us everywhere. I got away from him eventually."

"There had to be something about him that made you stay, Mom. Why else would you put up with that abuse?"

"Well, he was good in bed," she laughs.

"There it is." I hang my head and sigh out loud. "Thanks for that, Mom."

"And he was really funny sometimes," she adds.

"He had a good sense of humor?" I ask, trying to pull something positive from the conversation.

"Yes, and he was a stripper at the hotel down the road too, and a really good breakdancer."

"Wait. What? My father was a breakdancing stripper? Are you kidding?"

How do I even process this information? I can't help but awkwardly laugh. "Oh, my Gosh. I don't know whether to laugh or cry."

Can this story get any worse?

I suppose if I had to inherit any of my father's traits, having a good sense of humor and good dancing skills will do.

I straddle a fine line between mercy, grace, grief, and anger when talking with my mom. I'm upset with what she tells me, but I also feel sorry for what she went through. Emotional turbulence. The harrowing memories she shares with me about her childhood make me wonder who little Annie Andrews is, the trapped girl banging on the walls of her heart and mind.

I knew my mother was a depressed paranoid schizophrenic, but what I didn't know is that her mother *and* her grandmother were as well. Three generations of schizophrenia. The mental disorder isn't always genetically passed from one generation to the next; however, it can develop if triggered by traumatic events, and from what I know, there were a whole lot of them.

"What was your relationship like with your dad, my grandfather, growing up?" I've never met him and wonder if Mom can tell me about him.

"We didn't get along because he drank a lot, and the alcohol made him angry. My mother was furious with him because of it, but he used to hit her when she complained. He beat up our dog too. I only lived with him until I was five years old."

"Did he ever hurt you?"

"Not that I can remember. We were always moving because he couldn't pay the rent. My grandmother, Lillian, told me about my father bringing the landlords into our apartment and using my mother as a form of payment for rent. My mother was also sleeping with the man who lived in the apartment beneath us. She took me with her and the man tied me up in another bedroom so they could have privacy. When the man fell asleep, my mother untied me and told me not to tell my father."

"Oh, Mom."

I feel like I don't have the right to be angry toward Mom when I hear her say things like this. I feel like I'm far above the earth, walking an emotional tightrope with Mom's story. The weight of her trauma falls on me like a heavy rainfall and makes me slip. Her pain is like a wind that blows against my chest and pushes me further from the edge of safety. I feel unbalanced, out of control, and afraid. I could fall at any moment. Then there are feelings of compassion toward the little girl who endured witnessing her mom's body being sold for rent while she was helplessly tied up, unable to save the woman she loved. Flashbacks sting my side, and I remember Mom doing similar things to me. *God, tell me how to feel.*

"I remember the piles of beer cases stacked to the ceiling," Mom continues. "I felt sorry for my mother. My dad sold the landlord's appliances, left the place, and moved us into an abandoned home. We were very poor. I wore my father's dirty socks as mittens in the wintertime and had to search for snails in the backyard for soup."

"I didn't know your dad was like that, Mom. You don't talk about him very much. I know why now. I'm glad I never met him either. I'm sorry you had to see him drinking and hurting your mom. Also, I never knew you and your parents were unhoused."

"I don't really like talking about that part of my childhood," she says, lowering her head.

"It's not an easy thing to talk about, Mom." I clear my throat. "It's not an easy thing for me to hear either."

"I know. I'm sorry, Lainie. We don't have to talk about it."

"No, I appreciate you telling me. I want to hear it. It's just hard." I yawn. I'm utterly exhausted. I use my hand to support my head as I lean on it for support. My aching body feels locked. "It's a lot for me, Mom, but I'm okay," I lie. "Keep going."

"Okay. My mother couldn't take any more of my father's behavior and had a full-on mental breakdown. A doctor diagnosed her with schizophrenia and sent her to live in a psychiatric hospital.

That's when the children's aid took me and put me and Steve into foster care."

"How old were you then?"

"I was five years old and stayed until I was nine."

Nine years old—the age Mom gave me away with a single phone call. I swat the painful memory away and stay focused on her. "Where did you go when you were nine?"

"My grandmother, Lillian, sent a taxi to the foster home to pick me up but left my brother, Steve, there. I was surprised. Steve wasn't there when I left, and I didn't get to tell him I was leaving."

I didn't get to say good-bye to my siblings either.

"Why did your grandmother pick you over your brother?" I ask. I'm caught in the irony of the question. *Why did Mom choose to send me away over my other siblings?*

"She couldn't take both of us, because she was old. Steve started acting out after I left, and the foster home sent him away to a reform school for boys."

"How long did you live with your Grandma Lillian?"

"From nine to twelve years old. She took a nasty fall one night while walking uphill to the high school where she worked as a cleaner. She broke both her arms and was unable to work. Shortly after her fall, she had a heart attack. I was sent back into foster care when I was twelve."

"My goodness. Both your grandmothers were seriously injured."

"I know. They had bad luck. When I was nine, my father fell fifty feet while washing windows and broke every bone in his body. He was really depressed and became an even angrier man. He was on worker's compensation, drinking constantly, and betting his money on the horses."

"Bad luck is right. Your family broke enough bones for all generations to come. Did you stay in the foster home you were in for a long time?"

"No. I lost count of the number of foster homes I was in past twelve years old."

"Lost count? There were that many?" I'm shocked to hear about the number of homes my mother wasn't welcomed in. I'm heartbroken over the layers of rejection, abandonment, and shame we both repeatedly felt in our lives. I've never taken the time to get to know my mom like this. I feel somewhat guilty for waiting so long, but also know I wasn't ready for these details before now.

"I don't know why they moved me so much. It made me feel unwanted and unlovable."

"I understand that. Foster care made me feel that way too, Mom," I blurt out. I wonder if she understands the depths of trauma she caused by repeating history.

Mom tells me a vulnerable and disturbing story of the first time her body is violated. My heart bleeds for my 15-year-old mother who was simply walking through town when three men with selfish desires coerce her into their car and overpower her. This traumatic event is the first falling domino that forces the continuation of Mom's backward fall—a fall that is never caught by the supportive hands of another.

Months later, when Mom finally finds the courage to tell her foster parents what happened, they kick her out of their home and tell her they don't want to be associated with her filth.

At the age of seventeen, Mom returns to live with her grandmother but stays only a year because of her deteriorating health.

At eighteen, Mom meets her first husband, Lonnie Sr., and immediately becomes pregnant with Colleen. She delivers Colleen in 1974, Lonnie Jr. in 1975, and Rachel in 1976. Three kids in three years. Lonnie Sr. leaves Mom and their three toddlers for a teenage girl he meets. During one of their arguments over his cheating, he slams Mom's head against the apartment door. "He apologized, but I never forgot it." Mom says.

Mom was a tall, attractive young woman with baby-smooth skin, and a thin-lipped, full-cheeked smile. Her laugh was infectious. She yearned for a love she did not experience and showed her pain like a tattoo on her forehead. There's an unending list of people who broke her trust and stole her innocence. Her future could have been so different had she not been abandoned, neglected, and mistreated by her mother, father, foster parents, boyfriends, ex-husband, and herself. My future could have been different had she not caused those things in my life too.

Men like Marco and Matteo draw themselves to Mom like a magnet to metal. She's the perfect victim. She's vulnerable and alone without family support or protection. She's easily coerced, controlled, and manipulated. They feel entitled to her welfare money, her apartment, her family's food, her attention, and her time, but mostly they feel entitled to her body, which is how I and my siblings Blaire, Dylan, and Ellie are born.

I suggest it's time for bed. My mind and body are overwhelmed, and I need rest. Mom does too. I know it took a lot of courage to share what she's kept inside for decades. I walk mom downstairs to the guest bedroom and pray protection over her mind and against any spiritual warfare in our home. After saying goodnight, I head upstairs and sink into the safe arms of Levi in our bed, who's in a deep, peaceful slumber. I express my gratitude to God for mom's health, the blessings of family, home, and marriage, and ask for peace from my anxious mind. I slowly drift into the most pleasant dream, the furthest thing from the nightmares I'm accustomed to.

✦

CHAPTER TWENTY-SIX

Dreaming of My Inner Child

2018

S he's still here, the dirty abandoned girl living within me—still here in the place I left her long ago, alone and dreaming of a better life. I want to see her again.

I'm in a place of healing and rest, a place to let go, a place to heal. The cool spring air blows like a whisper across my skin, like soft silk flowing through strands of my dark, wavy hair, and, finally, like a sweeping touch along the tail of my rippling sundress. I'm laughing, running through a field of wildflowers that are proudly facing their petals toward the descending sun, the light that gives them life. I make myself a crown of flowers and continue my journey. I stop at the edge of the mountainside and look out to the still waters below me. I feel the embrace of my shadow as the warm sun kisses my face.

I gasp and hold my breath when I hear her call out our name. I am undone when I turn and see her weakened, small frame walking toward me with small, dirty hands grazing the weeds on either side of her. She looks away from me and lowers her head. Her clumpy hair falls to her face. Standing in front of me is the eight-year-old girl living within me.

Look up, sweetheart.

I kneel before her and place my soft hands under her smooth, round chin to support her face. I wait patiently for her to raise her glassy eyes from the weeds to mine. I can't escape her eyes.

I see her. I see myself. I see the pain in her eyes that cries out for a mother, a father, anyone to love her. I see her as a baby, crying aloud, begging for anyone to hold and comfort her. She looks at my lips as I speak softly to her.

Little girl, I'm sorry. What happened to you is not your fault. Please, forgive them. Forgive me. Let me hold you.

Tears escape the corners of her big brown eyes, leaving a clean, wet trail down her dirty cheeks. I explain to her how far I've come in my life and the journey I am still traveling. I apologize for not taking her with me and for leaving her alone for so many years. I cup her face and use my thumbs on either side to swipe her tears downward. I grasp her small hands and whisper, *I'm taking you with me this time. You will never be alone again.*

Our journey together is about to begin. She reaches for my hand and looks out to the water past the cliff. While it feels freeing to be on top of the world, I know a single gust of wind is all it takes to push us over the edge and into the valleys below. God, please protect us.

CHAPTER TWENTY-SEVEN

Baby Grace

2018

Levi has always been aware of my deep passion for foster care, and he is fully supportive of our family's pursuit of this mission together. We believe in providing children with a home filled with safety, security, stability and love, qualities both Levi and I are committed to offering. We complete the grueling process of becoming officially approved foster parents in June - a process that involves undergoing personally invasive interviews, comprehensive data collection about various aspects of your life, home studies, and months of training.

My faith in God, a committed community, and considerable inner work, has helped me overcome adversity in my life, and I want to offer the same faith, support, and sense of community to the children in my home. I have a burning desire for justice, and hold empathy, sensitivity, hope, and love for everyday people in my heart. I'm certain my personal experience as a child in foster and kinship care will help me to nurture the uniqueness of the children's needs in my home. It's not my intention to replace a child's family or diminish their significance. I firmly believe children belong with safe families. My commitment is to love them unconditionally, without judgment, and to provide the same nurturing care I longed for as a child.

I answer a call from our fostering agency in July 2018.

"Hi, Lainie. I have a possible placement for you if you're interested in learning more."

"Of course. How can I help?"

"There's a baby girl who's been in the intensive care unit at the hospital for the past three weeks and is ready to be released."

"A little girl? How sweet. What's her name?"

"She doesn't have one yet."

"No name? Mom must be having a hard time deciding," I joke.

"Her mother is no longer with us."

"She left the hospital?"

"She's passed away."

"Oh, I'm sorry." I pause and wait for her to cut the tension by saying something, but she doesn't. "When were you thinking of placing her?" I finally ask.

"Do you have a car seat? You can come this afternoon."

"This afternoon?"

"Preferably before four p.m."

"Wow. That's quick. Okay. Can I call my husband first? I'll need to get a few things to care for a baby."

"Yes, but we'll need to know soon. Also, she was born addicted—only weighed two pounds at birth. But she's been weaned with medication. She'll need special formula and bottles. The hospital will supply you with enough to get you started."

I cover my mouth and bulge my eyes.

"Lainie?"

"Yes. Sorry. Addicted?"

"She's four pounds now and off of the medication, so you don't have to worry."

"Okay." I don't want to say anything that will make me sound incompetent.

"Call me back if you have any questions after you've spoken to your husband," she says.

I take a moment to process the phone call and call Levi, who is supportive of the decision to welcome another little girl into our home. I sit down and begin to weep for this nameless baby who's without her mother. I whisper a prayer through tears.

"God, I'm sorry for what's happened to this baby girl's mother. I pray you're up there holding her and watching over her little girl together. Please let her know that I will love her baby and take good care of her. Make beauty out of these ashes, Jesus. Help me and everyone involved to navigate this heartbreaking process with compassion and grace. Use me to love this little girl for however long you need."

Our worker calls back, and I let her know we're willing to care for the preemie. She suggests we come the next day to give us more time to prepare. I'm thankful for that. The next morning, I strap the base of the car seat into my SUV, clip the bucket seat into it, and head to the hospital. I take the elevator up to the birthing floor. I'm so nervous. My heart bangs against the walls of my chest as I approach the doors of the neonatal intensive care unit. I gather my thoughts and ring the entry buzzer.

"What are you doing, Lainie?" I whisper to myself.

Once I'm let in, my worker and the nurse in charge meet me in the waiting room and bring me into a small, separate meeting room. They can tell I'm anxious. The nurse warns me that the child's grandmother, who is here holding the baby in a hospital room, is very upset about what's about to happen.

Of course she is.

The nurse in charge gives me an immense amount of information in a very short time and then asks whether I have any questions. I have a million, but I ask only the two holding microphones in my mind.

"Why isn't her grandmother taking her?"

"The agency won't be placing the baby with her." I want to ask why, but I don't.

"What about the father?"

"The man who claims to be the father is sure it's him, but we're waiting on DNA tests to confirm that."

The nurse gets up and swings the door open. I guess this means our meeting is over. She proceeds through the double doors and leads us to the pods. "Are you ready?"

"I really don't want to hurt Grandma's feelings," I mutter nervously.

My entrance is going to tear her heart to pieces. I see her swaying back and forth in the rocking chair, holding a tiny body in a pink blanket. The grandmother has long, dark, curly hair; small, dark eyes; and a thin, long nose that holds her rectangular-framed glasses. She's smiling into the eyes of the only part of her daughter she has left. Her expression is a mix of joy and pain as she strokes the baby's cheek. She is grieving, and I don't want to disturb her. I follow the nurse into the room. *Go easy, nurse. Please.* "Rita, this is Lainie. She's the foster mother that will be taking the baby home today."

Wow. What an introduction. She might as well introduce me as the baby thief.

Rita presses the baby tighter to her chest and looks as though her heart has stopped. Panic shoots from her eyes into mine. They are screaming with pain. It gives me chills. Her daughter has just died, and here I am, walking into the room with a nervous half-smile, holding a car seat to take her granddaughter. I don't know how to act.

"Hello." I say, softly. "I'm sorry."

Rita becomes angry and full of emotion. *Oh, God. She's gonna blow.* I understand her anger and prepare to be yelled at. She has every right to express the way she's feeling. She doesn't know me. She doesn't trust me. How can I blame her? I only need to put myself in her shoes for a second to feel a sliver of the pain she feels. I want to run out of the room. I want to snap my finger and make all this better.

"This is wrong! So very wrong!" her voice breaks. "I'm her grandmother. She should be coming home with me! She is the only part of my Tara I have left, and you're going to take her from me? My daughter just *died!* This is wrong. She needs to be with me. It isn't this girl's job to have my grandbaby." Her strong posture breaks into a slouch. She closes her eyes and drops her head as she cries onto her sleeping granddaughter. She pulls the glasses from her face, making her hair swing forward.

The nurse calmly says, "I think it would be good for Lainie to feed the little girl now so she can figure out how to put these special bottles together once she's home." *She dismissed her feelings.* I can't imagine someone taking my girls from me. I wonder whether my mother felt this way when she gave me away.

"I'd like to have a minute with Rita alone, if that's okay?"

I bravely ask the nurse and the worker to kindly leave the room. To my surprise, they agree.

Without anyone listening in, I apologize to Rita for the situation she's in. "This is not the way it's supposed to be. I know how wrong this feels, and I'm sorry your heart is hurting." I ask her whether it's okay to share my story with her so she knows who her grandbaby is staying with. She lifts her chin and looks into my eyes. I share the pain of being taken from my mother and being placed into foster care. I tell her of my mother's mental illness and what life was like for me and my siblings on the streets of Toronto. "I know how important it is for this sweet girl to be with her family. Being reunified with my family was all I ever wanted, and living without them was excruciating. I don't want that for any of you. I want you to be together." I reach for her hand. "My only job is to love her while you figure out the details. I promise you I will love her the way she deserves."

"You have children?" Rita asks through tears.

"Yes, two beautiful little girls who I know will love her too."

"Is your mom okay now?"

"She is." I smile. "Medication changed her life."

Rita reminds me so much of my mother. I see the pain of a mother who's lost her way and has consequently lost her children to the system. Rita squeezes my hand and apologizes for getting angry with me. She's glad I'm on her side. She likes that I have daughters of my own and that my intentions are to reunify her family. She shares her struggle of raising her own children with the involvement of CAS. She fears she won't be allowed in her grandkids' life because of her battle with her own mental health.

Her glossy eyes tell a story—a story I understand. I see fear, hopelessness, and loss. She loosens her grip on the pink bundle and passes the baby to me. I hold the nameless sleeping baby in front of me so we can both admire her features. I ask Rita to tell me everything the baby likes and what she doesn't. She explains how she likes to be held, how she likes her diaper to be changed (while the changer sings), and how she likes to sleep swaddled. I love her proud advice and how we're working to build trust. I don't want to be her enemy. I want to see her for who she is.

"Can you tell me about Tara?" I ask.

I can almost see the movie of Tara's childhood playing behind the tears forming in the corners of Grandma's eyes. Pain emerges from the smile she's trying to wear as she remembers her daughter. "She was beautiful," she begins. She struggles to form her next words. "She was also very sick. Her choices cost her her life, but I know the heart of my daughter." She pauses and releases a long-awaited exhalation. "I miss her so much. People don't feel comfortable talking about her because of what happened, but I want her to be remembered for who she was, not for what she did."

I notice the nurse and my worker on the other side of the Plexiglas wall, animating their conversations with their hands as they pack the supplies I need higher and higher into the empty car seat.

I focus my attention. "Rita, I'm really sorry about Tara. I can't imagine losing a child, no matter their age. I'm sorry for the way she passed and for the double loss you're going through now."

She rubs my arm. "I'll show you a picture of her on my phone." She pulls up a photo of Tara, and my heart sinks. The young woman clearly needed help. "This was her funeral photo. It's one of the only pictures we have of her. She was so sick. I hate everything about the way she died. I wish she had gotten help."

I sigh. "I'm sorry. Losing our way in life is easy; finding our way back seems too hard sometimes. I can see in your eyes how much you love and miss her."

She closes her phone. "I wasn't the best mother."

I think about the decisions Mom made that hurt me. "Neither was mine, but surprisingly, it never changed my love for her. I'm sure Tara loved you."

We sit together for a few moments in silence.

"Do you mind if I ask you a question?" I'm nervous.

"Sure," Rita says.

"This little girl doesn't have a name yet, and she's almost a month old. I know you have a name you want to call her, and so does the other side of her family. I really don't want to hurt anyone's feelings on either side. I was wondering if I could call her Grace until things get sorted out?" I'm worried that I'm out of line—that I've offended her. I want to take back my question.

After a pause, Rita answers, "I think it would be nice for the time being. She deserves to have a name."

The workers enter the room to see the two of us sitting close together, admiring Grace.

"Looks like you two had a chance to get to know each other better," my worker says, smiling.

After a quick lesson on how to use and sterilize preemie bottles for feeding, it's time to buckle Grace into her car seat and say good-bye. I assume I'm saying good-bye to Rita in the parking lot downstairs, but the staff escort her out of the building before me for safety reasons. I'm saddened. She's not a criminal. I understand it's protocol to do that; however, I can't imagine how the frail, brokenhearted woman is feeling.

I'm honored to love Grace and have her in our home, but I'm confused about the way I feel. How can one feel as if one is doing the right thing while being completely disheartened at the same time? I buckle Grace's car seat into my SUV and smile at her. I can't wait to introduce her to all the people who love our family. I know they'll love her too.

I've barely slept since Grace has been in our home. I'm a nervous wreck. *Is shaking a side effect of withdrawal, or is she cold? Is it a seizure? Why is she sneezing so much? Is it a cold or a side effect from withdrawal? Why does her body feel locked? Why does she spit up so much? Is she keeping enough formula down? Does she have some sort of reflux disease?* I am worried all the time. Grace needs to be fed every two hours, and the bottle sterilization and preparation process takes forty minutes. There are so many tiny parts to her bottles, including tiny white flaps that have to be placed perfectly to prevent Grace from swallowing too much air. With little sleep at night, and with two lively little girls that constantly need Mommy too, I am exhausted.

Grace is a champ. The next six weeks pass, and I'm able to get into the rhythm of being a mom to three little ones. The girls and I enjoy dressing Grace with pretty little dresses and frilly headbands. We love taking pictures of her, but for privacy reasons, we can't share them on social media. My girls giggle every time they hear her burp or pass gas, and it makes me laugh to see how funny they think it is. We get to see her first smiles, and we cheer when the doctor says she's gaining weight or reaching milestones.

Grace has weekly appointments at the hospital to make sure she's developing appropriately. Both sides of Grace's family make every effort to be present for her appointments. Sometimes Joe, the potential father's side, comes to meetings. Other times, the mom's side comes. Sometimes both sides show up and sit on opposite sides of the room. *This is so awkward.* Both sides are pursuing kinship custody, so I stand against the wall between them to stay neutral. I care for them all and only want what's best for Grace. Joe shows me pictures of Tara during one of Grace's appointments. He quickly swipes past a few that make me gasp and close my eyes. He tells me why he loves her and shares his favorite memories with her. He shows me the tombstone he's chosen for her grave site—a mother angel holding her baby.

On top of all the hospital appointments, Grace has visits three times a week at the agency. I feel like a taxi service. I enjoy seeing her family and getting to know them better. It's nice to have the constant support and reassurance from them that I'm caring for Grace the way I promised I would.

The phone rings, and I race around the house trying to follow the noise. I find the phone buried under a pile of laundry and quickly pick it up to read an unknown number.

"Hi, Lainie. It's Sue from the Children's Aid Society. The paternity tests are in; Joe is the father."

This is how it ends.

"Court has just finished, and the judge has granted custody to

Joe's eldest daughter, Ashley, and her husband, Harley. How fast can you get here with Grace?"

I fall to my knees and hang my head. I pinch the bridge of my nose with my thumb and pointer finger and rock myself slowly for comfort. Violet and Olivia kneel before me. "Mommy, why are you crying?"

I bring my finger to my mouth and close my eyes, forcing my silent tears to fall to my lap. "Shh … It's okay, girls. Go play for a minute, okay?" I know it's time for our darling girl to return home with her family, but I wasn't expecting the pain of grief and loss to squeeze my heart this suddenly.

"Um, I … um, I'm home with the girls. Levi's not home from work yet. I just need some time to … I need to pack up her things. I'm not prepared. I need to get the girls ready."

"Lainie," the worker begins. "I want you to know how sorry I am. I know this is hard for you. Both sides of the family have told me several times about how much they adore you. It has been such a pleasure working alongside you. Joe and Ashley want you to know how much they appreciate all you've done for Grace and know how much you love her. I have been doing this job for fifteen years, and I can honestly say I've never met a foster parent like you. Truly, it's been a pleasure."

"Thank you for saying that. It means a lot to me. I can try to be there in an hour …"

"If you could make it before then, that would be great. The agency is closed now, and I need to get going. The family is waiting outside for her."

How sweet she was only a moment ago, only to tell me her workday is over, and she wants to go home. I race around the house crying, throwing Grace's belongings into a plastic bin. There is so much pressure behind my eyes from holding in the brimming explosion of pent-up air during the call. I can barely see through my tears.

"Mommy, who was it? Why are you crying?" Violet asks.

"It's time for baby Grace to go home, sweetheart. Remember we talked about how Grace might go live with her sister?"

"I don't want her to go, Mommy. I want her to stay here with us."

"I know, baby. Can you be a big girl and help Mommy gather up Grace's things?"

"What about Daddy? He's not home to say good-bye."

"You're right, honey. We'll call him on the way there, okay?"

I need more time: more time to explain to our little girls why Grace is leaving, more time to prepare, more time with Grace. I wish for Levi to be home. I want him to hold me.

"Let's get in the car, girls, okay? Mommy will buckle you up."

"Can you turn the music on for baby Grace so she doesn't cry because she's leaving us? It'll make her feel better, Mommy."

"Sure, sweetheart. That's really nice of you."

Their innocence is so pure. *How blessed am I to have this much love in my life?* I listen to the girls as they sing softly to Grace one last time. I feel joy and loss, pain and love, weakness and strength, all at the same time.

Grace's family is waiting on the sidewalk smiling when we arrive at the agency. I park the car and get out to open the rear passenger door, where Grace's car seat is. I try to avoid eye contact with the family because I want to appear strong. They're so joyful, and I don't want to ruin their excitement. If I look at them, I'll fall apart. I pull Grace from her car seat and hand her to Joe and Ashley with a weak smile. They both look into my eyes and pull me into an embrace.

"Thank you, Lainie. For all you've done for my daughter." Joe says. "We were so scared in the beginning when they told us she'd be going into foster care, but you made this process so much easier for us. Tara would have been glad she was with you."

Tara, I think. *I'm sad you're not here.*

"Thanks, Joe. That means a lot. It's been amazing getting to know you and your family. I'm really happy for you. This is what we've been fighting for, right? The day has finally arrived for her to join her family." I rub the side of Grace's cheek. "I have no doubt she's going to have an amazing life and be totally loved by all of you. Thank you for believing in me and trusting me with your daughter. Our family will miss her terribly."

"We hope it doesn't end here, Lainie. We want you to still be in her life if you're okay with that. We want you to be there for her birthdays and life's milestones. You'll always be an important part of her life."

Those words bring me such peace. I hug them all one more time, then lean down to Grace's car seat and give her a kiss on her forehead.

"Bye, sweet girl. We'll miss you."

I watch Joe and Ashley walk away with Grace, smiling at each other. Grace has been given a new name today that suits her perfectly. I am so happy, even though my heart is broken. I get back into my car and lean my head over the steering wheel. I offer up a broken prayer. I thank God for the life I've lived as a foster child, for the unique perspective it's given me as a foster parent, and for the abundance of love I have in my heart for kids who need a home. I thank God for Grace's family and ask him to give Tara a big hug for me. Her baby is going to be just fine.

I drive out of the parking lot and head toward home. I look into the rearview mirror to see my girls sitting quietly together, processing all that's happened. Then I hear a little singing voice:

"You give and take away.

You give and take away.

My heart will choose to say,

Lord, blessed be your name."

It is one of the most touching moments my heart has ever encountered. My heart is overflowing with an abundance of emotions. The lyrics are beautiful and exactly what I need to hear, but what feels even more beautiful is how God spoke them through the mouth of my five-year-old firstborn daughter, who is holding the hand of her little sister.

CHAPTER TWENTY-EIGHT

Fostering Trauma

2018

I accept a substitute assignment at a local school on October 31, 2018, Halloween. *I know why the educational assistants called in sick today.* The kids in the classroom are hyped up on sugar, running around, and being loud—so loud I need to take my hearing aids out. It's rained all day, which means all three recesses are indoors. The teacher tries to keep the students under control, but it's nearly impossible. At the end of the workday, I bolt down the hallway and out the front doors of the school as if I'm an Olympic walker. Oh, it's also pouring outside, and I've forgotten my umbrella.

Water drips down my nose and into my lap as I sit wet and shivering in my SUV. I pull the visor down in front of my face to look in the mirror and laugh. What a mess I am. I reach for the baby wipes in the glove box to swipe away the black trails of mascara running down my cheeks. I blast the hot air, turn on the heated seats, and start the podcast I've been trying to listen to for weeks.

I'm on my way to order myself a latte from a local coffee shop, something I enjoy drinking after a long workday, without the sound of screaming children in the backseat. My phone rings, interrupting my podcast. "Come on!" I moan, annoyed at being robbed of down time. When I realize it's Carrie, my favorite worker from another fostering agency, I answer in a cheerful voice, as if I didn't just yell into the air two seconds earlier. She asks whether we can take an emergency placement into our home—a one-year-old boy and a three-year-old girl.

"I need to know rather quickly, Lainie, if you and Levi can take these kids. It's a bit of an emergency."

"What's the emergency? What do I need to know?"

"Well …" She pauses. "This is one of the worst cases, and you're my first phone call."

"You must have a lot of faith in me," I joke nervously.

"I do. These two kids were just found in a locked bedroom with boarded up windows, naked and freezing. I'm not sure how long they've been in there for, but neither of them can talk. There was a large plastic sheet covering a plywood floor full of feces and urine from the last several weeks. They were just … covered in it, Lainie. It's just terrible. I know it's a lot to ask of you and Levi, and your girls. We need a place for them to go until we can figure out other arrangements. They're going to need a lot of support."

"Carrie," I forcefully say in disbelief. "I'll do whatever I can to help those kids. Bring them to me. I'm sure Levi will be on board, but I'll give him a call to make sure."

"I can be at your place in an hour."

"An hour?" I ask, surprised.

"Yes, they're in the workers' car right now. We'll help you as much as we can with the supplies you'll need. They have no belongings with them."

"Okay, I'm heading home now. I'm nervous, Carrie. I'll call you right back after I talk to Levi."

"You'll do great, Lainie. I believe in you."

Memories of my childhood begin to fall on me like the relentless downpour on my windshield, blurring my vision and crowding my mind. I watch the wipers frantically swipe back and forth, back and forth, back and forth. Oh, how they remind me of my life; every time I try to sprint forward to escape the pain of my past, I am whipped back into time and forced to relive the memories over and over again. I grip the steering wheel tighter.

I reminisce about my younger self sitting naked and covered in my own waste while Mom watches the TV, not paying attention to me. I recall the hunger pains—how my stomach grumbled for food. The child within me isn't sure she can handle the reflection of her own trauma. I can feel her within me. I can hear her crying out in frustration.

"You're safe," I whisper to myself.

I call Levi and tell him what I've just agreed to, and of course he's supportive. It's raining today, so he's heading home early. I stand in anticipation at my front door, waiting for the kids to arrive. Several protection workers' cars begin to line my small street, including Carrie's. Two workers walk up to my door, each carrying a child.

"Can I help you bring anything in?" I ask.

"There's nothing to bring in."

"Right … Okay, come in," I say, holding the door open.

It's freezing outside, and the kids have no shoes or coats on. *This feels familiar.* The diapers and onesies they're wearing have been given to them by the agency. *This does too.* I arrived at my foster home the same way. Anna, the three-year-old girl, is already asleep from utter exhaustion and enters my house first. Her matted, chestnut-brown hair looks as though it's been chopped at the roots with rusty scissors. Some strands are short; others, quite long. I lead the worker to our spare room, where they lay her down in a small, single bed. She sleeps with her chest to the mattress, her elbows pulled under her body and her hands in fists beneath her chin. I see myself in the way she sleeps. I sit on the floor with my chin on the edge of her bed, take in her facial features and stroke her hair. She sleepily opens her eyelids and reveals her dark brown eyes. She has the longest eyelashes I have ever seen on a child. Her cheeks are smooth and full, the same way mine are, and she has a small button nose. I rub her back and pull a blanket from the drawer beneath the bed. She turns her face away from me as I tuck her in.

I leave the room to meet Easton, the one-year-old boy, who is crying and confused from all that's happening. His curly blonde hair dangles down his forehead and covers his blonde eyebrows. Tears fall from his big brown eyes and down his jaundiced cheeks, and boogers run from his small nose into his trembling mouth. The worker hands him to me. He rests his head on my shoulder, and I hold him a little tighter. I can smell the feces on his skin and scalp. I want to cry but hold myself together. *How could anyone do this to a child?* I rub his back and rock him side to side. I look at the workers, hoping they'll tell me something that makes sense. They hand me two binders of information and give me a general recap of what they've witnessed that day. There is so much information. I am completely overwhelmed and feel as if I'm on the verge of a panic attack. I am running on pure adrenaline. I am mentally matching the kids' information in column A to the similarities of my childhood in column B. I am angry at these kids' parents and the neglectful decisions they've made. I'm angry at my mother all over again. Before the worker leaves, she tells me the agency will be in contact with me shortly to set up parental visits with the kids. I am fuming inside.

Did I hear her right? How could the parents possibly be allowed to see these babies after what they've done? They should be in jail.

Again I am reminded of my mother's neglect, but I remember that even after all I went through, I just wanted to be with her. I have a tug-of-war feeling about seeing both sides of foster care. It feels strange to be an adult, to see myself in the eyes of children. I am not normally so quick to judge, but I'm angry and disgusted at the neglect. I wonder how many people thought of my mother the same way I think of these children's parents.

Jane, my ever-supportive neighbor, is here getting our girls into their Halloween costumes and is taking them out trick-or-treating for us. Anna and her brother are in dire need of a bath. I run the warm water into our shallow almond-colored tub and add liquid bath soap for white mountains of bubbles. I bring Anna and Easton to the bathroom and help them undress. Anna is making babbling noises to her wiggling fingers. Easton is still crying. The foul smell escaping every pore of their bodies makes my stomach weak. I scrape feces from the bottoms of their feet and ankles with a body cloth but can't get their feet clean. I realize their skin is stained from months of walking in their own waste. I place them both into the tub. Anna is unaffected by her brother's painful cries, but I feel every wound in his breaking voice. I am overwhelmed, brokenhearted, and angry for these children. I apply tea tree oil shampoo to their heads and scrub their matted hair. I let it sit for a few minutes and then rinse it off and repeat the process. A black cloud of head bugs floats on the surface of the dirty water. I begin to cry. I feel as though I'm taking care of my younger self. It feels strange to be a foster mother to a child who resembles me so much.

The next day is cold and miserable outside. Anna and Easton need warm clothes and winter attire for the season immediately. I load Violet, Olivia, Anna and Easton into my SUV and grumble to myself that I should have bought a van. My wipers push off the wet and heavy snow on my windshield. After a much slower and longer drive than it should have been, I arrive at the store and wait in the parking lot for Carrie. Anna is content and playing with her fingers, Easton is screaming at the top of his lungs, and my girls are both plugging their ears. I close my eyes, lean my head back, and wish I had stopped for a coffee.

I look into the rearview mirror and see Carrie heading toward me. I turn to face my four little passengers, all under the age of four, and tell them we need to unload quickly or we'll all be soaking wet and cold. I hop out of the driver's seat and fling the side door open. I climb into the car, lean over the middle row, and unbuckle Violet and Olivia from their car seats in the back. I pull them over Anna and Easton's heads and pass them to Carrie's open arms. Then I unbuckle Anna and Easton in the middle row, who are both barefoot and coatless, and guide them out of the car. I secure one on each of my hips, then kick the door closed and run into the store.

Carrie offers to hold Easton, who is red-faced, screaming, and flailing his arms and legs, while I frantically rip items from hangers and throw them into baskets. My daughters are trying to interact with Anna, who babbles to her fingers, neither impressed by the girls' efforts or aware of their presence. The store manager realizes what's going on and, upon checkout, graciously offers us the piles of clothes for half price. I feel anxious as the clerk slowly searches for each clothing tag. *Scan faster*, I think, "Are they all yours?" she asks. I look straight through her head, and don't even respond. Easton is now convulsing his body on the floor. Carrie's hair looks as if she's been electrocuted. Olivia is sucking her thumb by the front door. Violet's chatting up a storm with a staff member. Anna is unbothered, sitting with her legs crossed in the checkout lane. My heart is racing. I don't like that Olivia is standing so close to the door. She could be easily taken there. I yell for her to come stand by me, and for Violet to do the same. *Come on, lady*, I think. She's taking forever. I could be scanning the items faster. I want to take the scanning gun from her and do it myself. I want someone more experienced to take over. I'm sweating, tapping my debit card impatiently on the counter. I stare at the mountain of clothes on the counter and remember the piles of laundry I'm already behind on at home. Finally, she's done. "We'll cover the cost of these, Lainie." It's enough to make me cry. I grab the bags, push through the door of the store toward the car, and toss them into the trunk. "Mommy, you have white hair!" Olivia laughs.

"The snowflakes are so big today, honey."

Carrie helps me load all four kids back into my SUV. She gives me a hug, wishes me luck, and tells me to give her a call if I need anything at all. She leaves for her car, and an instant lump in my throat appears. I don't want to fall apart here. I have four kids to be responsible for now. "Everybody ready?" I ask. "Mommy, please make him stop crying!" Violet yells, covering her ears. She has audio processing disorder, and loud noises are extremely upsetting for her. "I'm sorry, sweet girl. I know this is hard. I'll find you a quiet space when we get home, okay?"

I pull out of the parking lot and head home.

"I've got this. I've got this. I've got this." I repeat the phrase, trying to hype myself up.

The next three weeks are the most difficult, grueling, exhausting weeks I have ever experienced with any foster children. Easton refuses to let me comfort him. His torturous screams cause my head to ring like a gong. I try to pick him up and hold him, but he contorts his body to get away from me. He refuses his food and whips it across the room. He bangs his face off the floor as he screams in frustration, and it breaks my soul. With tears running down my face, I put him in his crib and close the door so I can gather myself for a minute. Then I hear banging. I think he's kicking the spindles, but I'm wrong. I walk in and see him smashing his face against the edge of the wooden crib. He has blood all over his face and there are teeth marks engraved into the perimeter of the wood. My heart is broken. This sweet boy's needs weren't nurtured as a baby, and therefore he doesn't know that I'm safe or that I can help him. I just want to love him, but I feel completely useless.

Anna is in the garbage cupboard, eating the waste from meal prep. My instant, uncalculated reaction is to take the food from her. I feel horrible when I realize I've scared her. Her eyes are wide with fear as I approach her. Her dark brown eyes look black. "Anna, sweetheart. I'm sorry. Look, there's fresh food on the table. You don't have to eat from the garbage." I put my hand out for her to pass me the old food clutched in her fist, but she holds it close to her chest and bends over to protect it. She quickly shoves it into her mouth before I can stop her. I bring her to the table, where there's fresh fruit and granola bars available, and show her she can eat anytime she wants to. Instead of eating the food, she walks around the table and chomps its wooden edges with her teeth. I make my assumptions as to why she refuses to eat the food on the table and only from the garbage. Again, my heart is broken. I wish she could talk to me.

When I redirect Anna, she bangs her face on the floor and smashes the back of her head against the walls repeatedly. Easton copies his sister when she's upset and begins to bang his face too. I do my best to prevent them from hurting themselves and feel powerless that I can't. They rip their diapers off and defecate and urinate on the floor and carpets. Easton's clothes are constantly soiled, and my floor stinks horribly. I put his onesies on backward, but he still manages to take his diaper off while dressed, too. At mealtime, I sit them in their high chairs and feed them. They spit their food out and throw it across the room. They grab anything within reach to throw it off the table. I sit with spaghetti sliding down the side of my face while everyone screams. I am exhausted. Levi is working insane hours at two different jobs. He leaves for work before the kids wake in the morning and doesn't get home until after everyone has fallen asleep. I am alone and overwhelmed.

I feel like a failure. I can't help Easton or Anna the way they need. They need so much more than I give them. I can't keep up with all of their visits with their mother and her boyfriend and all of their appointments. They need speech and vision therapy. They need emotional, mental, and physical evaluations. They need experienced foster parents who can invest time into their rehabilitation.

After Anna and Easton fell asleep, I go into Violet's room to rock her to sleep. She asks, "Mommy, do you still love me?" I am shocked. She's only five years old. "Of course, I do, Violet. That makes me sad to hear you ask that. What makes you think I don't love you?"

"You don't play with me anymore, Mommy. You only help Anna and Easton and not me or Olivia anymore."

It completely breaks my spirit. I hold her close to me and sob. "I'm so sorry, sweetheart. You're right. I have been spending most of my time helping Easton and Anna. Mommy is tired, and I don't have much energy to play these days. Mommy is trying hard to make sure Easton and Anna stay safe.

"She bites me, Mommy, and hits me and scratches me."

"I'm sorry for that too, Violet. Mommy is trying to teach Anna to use gentle hands with you. She's learning. Anna doesn't know how to use her words yet. Mommy will try harder to keep you safe, okay? I do love you, Violet. I always will, no matter who comes to live with us."

Anna smiles for the first time, and I am overjoyed. The girls are holding her hands and dancing in a circle, singing a nursery rhyme. Anna throws her head back, laughing, and her smile lights up the room. She makes eye contact with the girls—something she hasn't done yet. I feel as if I'm witnessing a miracle. I laugh when she laughs, and then I cry tears of joy. I have waited weeks to see her smile and laugh. It is soul-filling to see her experience gleeful moments of delight. I stare at the three of them and breathe deep. Anna's had enough of playing. She leaves the circle and faces the wall, bouncing her bottom lip with her fingers while babbling to herself. I put my arms out to her, wondering whether she'll accept a hug from me. She turns her body away from mine and slowly backs into my arms. She lets me hold her for a few seconds, then goes to hide in the bedroom.

Carrie checks in on me frequently and shares her concern about the load I'm carrying. I cry into the phone in utter exhaustion with four kids crying in the background. "I can't go another day, Carrie. I can't. I haven't slept in weeks. They need so much more than I can give them. Easton hasn't stopped crying since the night he came here. I have tried my very best, and I feel like a failure. I never wanted anyone to give up on me when I was in foster care. I feel like I'm quitting on them."

"Lainie, this placement was only meant to be a night or two, a week at max, until we made other arrangements, but you wanted to keep going for them. I applaud your efforts, and so do the other workers within the agency. They're surprised you lasted this long, to be honest."

"I don't want to let them down, Carrie. Where will they go? They need an experienced foster home where they can be given the time and attention and help they need until their parents get sorted out."

"You leave that with me. Right now, I just want to make sure you're okay. I'm going to make some phone calls, and then I'm coming to you with a Starbucks, okay?"

"Thank you." I look down to my stretched shirt and wipe my dirty face with my sleeve. "I'll see you when you get here."

Carrie makes plans for Easton and Anna to be placed into the foster home of an older couple. They are empty nesters with decades of fostering experience and an abundance of resources and skills I don't have yet. I have equal feelings of sadness, guilt, and relief about ending their placement in our home, and I decide to take the next six months off to work through the secondary trauma I experienced during their placement. Some days, I cry alone behind my bedroom door because I miss them so much. Other days, their trauma eats me up inside and I'm thankful I made the right decision for them. I have peace and comfort knowing they're getting the professional help they need and deserve —the help I needed and deserved when I was their age.

CHAPTER TWENTY-NINE

Cooper

2019

In June 2019, I receive a call from the agency asking whether we can take in a newborn baby boy from the hospital. I call Levi right away to give him the little information I have, and of course, he is ready and willing to help. With familiar anxious feelings, I head to the hospital. A nurse grants me access into the maternity ward and leads me to the first birthing pod on the right.

A weary young mother looks down into the eyes of her son, knowing she'll soon be escorted from the hospital without her baby in her arms. She's hurting. She's been hurt. She's being hurt. Everything I see in her eyes tells me she deserves better than the life she's living; everything about her posture tells me she's defeated and has given up hope. I see it all over her, and it pains me to see her in this situation. I whisper a prayer: "God, heal the little girl within her. Help her to break free from the lies she believes about herself so she can fall in love with who she is and who you made her to be. Release her from the pain she carries. Give her hope, Jesus."

I quietly enter the nursing room and introduce myself.

She looks me up and down, then looks away. "I'm Jaymi," she responds quietly. She knows why I'm here, and she's not happy about it; I wouldn't be either. "This is Cooper," she says as she caresses her son's head and smooths his blanket. Jaymi looks like a makeup-free younger version of my mother, and it stirs my heart in ways I can't explain. I wonder whether Mom had the same fear in her eyes when they took Rosie and Hudson from her in the hospital.

"Can I sit with you?" I ask. She moves over. "Your son is beautiful, Jaymi." I glance from Jaymi's eyes to Cooper's. "How was your birth? Are you feeling okay?" She looks into my eyes. I wonder whether I'm the first person to ask. She tells me about her labor experience and Cooper's birth. She's silent for a moment, then wipes her eyes with the sleeve of her oversize black sweatshirt. "I'm really sorry, Jaymi." I rub her back and share the tears of a mother with her. "This isn't the way it's supposed to be."

"I'm not who he needs me to be."

The presence of the looming, waiting workers makes Jaymi uncomfortable. It's time. She lifts her son, kisses his cheek, and whispers her good-byes. She wipes her fallen tears from her son's face and passes him to me. Fighting postbirth pain, she slowly gets up, grabs her plastic grocery bag of belongings, and is escorted from the hospital.

Jaymi, I'm sorry.

The nurse notices my muffled breathing. I'm trying to hold back tears. "You're doing the right thing, Lainie," she says.

I shake my head. "I understand what you mean, but this doesn't feel right at all."

People praise foster parents. *What for?* I wonder. I hate the feelings I'm soaking in. This doesn't feel good or right or praiseworthy. It feels wrong and painful for everyone involved. Every foster and adoptive child's story begins with loss, and families look different because of this. I believe children belong in safe families, and safe families belong together. I realize how needed I am as a foster parent, and that's why I'm here, but I pray for the day I'm not needed in this way.

I pull Cooper close to my chest and breathe in the lingering scent of his mother's skin. I scan the hospital room one final time, wondering how many Jaymis have been in here before. I kneel to buckle Cooper into his car seat, then make my way through the automatic doors to the nursing station to sign out. Sadness and hope are twisted, like a rope, around my heart.

CHAPTER THIRTY

Reunited

2021

I gravitated toward the words written by my foster mother, Bee, in my CCAS file. My heart never forgot her or her family, and I wanted to find them and pursue a relationship if they would allow it. Thirty years ago, Bee knew the heart of my inner child, and I still felt connected to her. She held the missing memories I desperately craved. I wanted to know who I was and who she believed I would be. I wanted to make her proud and let her know I turned out okay. Putting my heart on the line and asking for a relationship with her was worth the risk of her possibly rejecting me.

The only information I had in my file was a photocopy of five first names signed on my fourth birthday card. Their last name had been redacted, which made my search for them feel impossible. I had the name of the agency they fostered me through thirty years prior, but because of privacy reasons, the agency couldn't help me.

I joined Facebook groups in the general area of where my foster home was and asked people whether they had any information regarding the names in the birthday card. In 2021, while finishing the first draft of this book, a lady sent me a private message saying she believed she had found who I was looking for. She had looked up their names on Facebook and searched their friends list. One of the names she searched had four family members with the same names as those on my card. I was excited and nervous. I reached out to Bee and three of my foster brothers through Facebook Messenger. When one of the brothers responded, "Hi Lainie! I remember you and your sister, Ellie. I'll let my mom know. You have found the right family!" I froze for a moment and then called Ellie. I couldn't believe he remembered us from over three decades ago. Bee responded to my message, and we FaceTimed each other. After talking for almost two hours, we decided to set a date for a backyard barbecue and pool party at her house—an hour and a half from where I lived with Levi and our children, and only a forty-five-minute drive from the Thompsons' house. It pained me to think that during the hardest years of my life, they were so close to me. If only I had known.

During our visit, Bee gave me and Ellie a picture album full of colored photos to replace the black-and-white ones that were nothing more than shadows in my foster care file. Bee gave me the gift of childhood memories, and it meant everything to me. I ran my fingers over each picture, smiling, seeing the evidence of joy in my childhood. What I saw beyond the pictures was a proud foster mom smiling behind a camera lens toward me, proud of who I was and attentive toward what I was doing and discovering.

Bee told us story after story of all she remembered about us, including stories of me jumping out of moving vehicles and coming home from visits with cockroaches squashed under my feet and bugs crawling in my hair. I clung to each word, no matter how gross the story was. Bee looked over and said, "We loved you. We would have adopted you girls in a heartbeat if it had been an option at the time."

"Really? I asked, moved by her words. Her desire to adopt me all those years ago releases abandonment's grip on me. *My life could have been so different.* "We didn't even get to say good-bye. You went for a visit one day in December and never came back home to us." *I know.* "We had your Christmas presents under the tree and no little girls to give them to on Christmas morning. I was devastated."

"Sorry," is all I whispered.

"I'm glad you found me. We have each other again."

I became quiet and reflected on our conversation. I looked out to the yard and saw my kids and Dee's grandchildren playing together. I fixed myself another plate of food and stuffed my feelings down with every bite. Grief ripped my heart out and gratitude embraced me; I may have missed out on something beautiful, but I was wanted.

That summer, Bee invited me and my children to her family's cottage—the same cottage I went to as a three-year-old foster child. I sat on the dock with Bee, enjoying a cold drink, watching my daughters and our foster son laugh and jump off the edge of the dock and into the water, making memories the same way I did three decades prior. In that very moment, I realized my life had come full circle. God's restorative redemption overwhelmed me. Tears rolled down my cheeks and joy filled my heart as I stood in awe of my children, and the beauty of God's creation. He made me, and he knows me. I'm wanted, I'm chosen, and I belong.

He turned the painful parts of a little girl's life into a love letter to his daughter.

EPILOGUE

"If you don't take her in, she'll be living in a homeless shelter this winter," Mom's worker tells me.

Flashbacks of finding Mom unhoused and nearly frozen under a streetlamp still haunt me.

I can't let that happen to her again.

Becoming Mom's caretaker after the traumatic life I endured with her wasn't something I saw for my future, but I had a stable home, a wonderful supportive family, and the space to accommodate her. When discussing solutions with my eight other siblings, I felt the urge and responsibility to say yes to Mom living with us.

Mom's learned helplessness and mental impairments makes her seem like a small child trapped in a senior's body. She depends on me for everything. I knew her moving in would be hard for my mental health and for my family and the changes they would have to become accustomed to. I had nightmares and panic attacks for weeks. I felt a churning emotional turmoil I couldn't manage. I cried all the time. I hid in my room. I couldn't sleep. I felt buried and burdened. I was drowning on the inside, and nobody seemed to understand the severity of the mental torture I was experiencing. I felt alone with my troubled thoughts. I was struggling with childhood trauma, and it was devouring my body and mind. Finally, after many private battles with God, he revealed the deepest, darkest question piercing my heart

Why should I have to care for the woman who neglected me? The woman who gave me away multiple times like I was nothing? I was a small, helpless child that deserved to be cared for too.

Like a pulled weed that won't die, abandonment, rejection, and shame sprouted their ugly heads. The irony of our situation felt so heavy on me, and no part of our situation felt fair. God still has work to do on my heart.

I hear God's gentle whisper: "Forgiveness."

Oh, that word. It gets stuck in my throat and burns my lips. It's a daily choice I make, but it's much harder to do with her living in my home.

Over time, I realize Mom needs the same things I needed as a small, helpless child. The little girl who was abandoned, neglected, and abused by her parents deserves to be loved too. It's not too late for her. She deserves to be cared for, have her needs met, and live the rest of her life in a home that feels safe. I've come to know that she and I are not so different after all. This life hasn't been fair to either of us, but we can start again. Our pasts do not have to predict our future.

My goal as a daughter is to be the caretaker my mom needed as a child. That's the redemption in our story. While our pasts were horrific, our futures don't have to be. We have lived enough of our lives with feelings too big for us to understand or handle. I'm trusting God with my big emotions, and I'm trusting him with Mom's future.

I have wept at the feet of Jesus for the life story he's given me and my mother, but I have peace knowing it won't continue in my family.

There are hurting families all over the world who need regular people like you and me to walk alongside them through this gut-wrenching process and tell them they're worth fighting for. We are wired for human connection and love, and if we all do that to our fullest potential, we can make a difference for everyone impacted by foster care.

Advocating for foster kids and their families is my future, and I want you to be a part of it. Many former foster youths are severely struggling with their mental health. Statistically, many of them are incarcerated, unemployed, unhoused, addicted to substances, pregnant before their nineteenth birthday, and falling victim to sex trafficking. They feel alone and without support. In the United

States, there are over four hundred thousand children living in the foster care system. In Canada, there are over fifty-nine thousand, with neglect being the reason for seventy percent of the system's placements. These numbers are significant and there's nothing simple about it.

ACKNOWLEDGMENTS

Thank you, Jesus, for your redeeming love, which fills me to the brink when I feel empty. Thank you for who *you* say I am, not what the world thinks of me, my mother, my family, or my experiences. I know who I am in you—a wanted and chosen daughter who belongs in your family and is loved unconditionally. When I forget the truth, help me to sit tall and straighten my crown.

Levi, thank you for keeping God at the center of our household and for leading our family with grace and strength. From that nervous front-porch kiss nearly two decades ago to the depth of love we share today, you have always been my rock, my confidant, and my partner in every sense of the word. I love being your wife and I'm filled with gratitude for your unwavering love and devotion. I fall more and more in love with you every day and I owe so much of my healing to you.

To my children, thank you for the whimsy and joy you bring to my life. Being your mother is a privilege that fills me with such pride and purpose. You are the reason I wake up every day and the inspiration behind my desire to be the best version of myself. I love you forever.

To my mom, and my siblings, Colleen, Lonnie Jr., Rachel, Blaire, Dylan, Ellie, Rosie, and Hudson, I'm eternally grateful for the hours we spent learning about each other's lives. I've gained a deeper empathy and understanding about our experiences, which has brought great healing to my life. Please grant me grace and forgiveness for anything I've written that falls short of your expectations. I love you, and I'm proud to call you family.

To my friend and mentor, Piper, thank you for seeing my strengths and never looking down on me with pity. I didn't want to write this book alongside someone who said, "Poor you," every other line. You're a "Dig deeper. Feel it all. Write it down," kind of person and it's exactly what I needed. You have taught me what it means to be authentic, and I feel fully known by you.

Here's a bit of our story:

New York Times bestselling author Bob Goff was running an online course for aspiring authors called the Dream Big Framework Writing Course in March 2020. It's where I met Piper Hill, a fierce, loyal, God-filled woman who believed in me and my story since my first submission in Bob's course.

Piper had plans to write her own book, but God put it on her heart to put her book aside to mentor me as I wrote mine. I couldn't fathom her putting her dream aside for me. I barely knew who she was, and trusting wasn't my forte. I had glimpses of who she was from her writing assignments and knew she lived in Florida, but that was about it. Everything in my life had come at a cost, and Piper wanted to help me for free. I felt better knowing that if she helped me and decided to quit when my story made her uncomfortable, I would never have to see her again.

After hours of sharing our stories over Zoom and FaceTime, I knew Piper was a woman I could trust. It was this message from her that confirmed it:

> Dear Lainie,
>
> I am writing to process what happened today. I heard your story as you read it to me, and I felt a depth of emotion I have not experienced in a long time. It was never pity or feeling sorry for you. As I sit on the other side of the computer screen, here is what I feel. It is so complicated, and I can't make a nice clean list to explain it but here is what I feel, and I think your readers will also experience.
>
> I feel …
>
> - An intense sadness for the way you were treated.
> - Incredible anger at those who hurt you.

- Fury at the egregious injustice that happened as programs that were meant to keep you safe only victimized you further.
- Grief for all the other people in your story who were also hurt and victimized.
- A sense of fierce protection for who you are now, that no one ever hurts you again.
- Incredible respect for your ability to not only survive but THRIVE.
- A humble disposition toward you, that you would trust me with your story and value my input.
- Deep, deep love for you as my sister in Christ.
- Thanksgiving to God that you were made stronger through your experiences but also an understanding that as you are weak, He is strong.

I cry tears with you, and I cry after we hang up. I am just processing. I am not crushed because you are not crushed. You inspire me so much and that is what actually makes it the hardest. Your ability to write a book that contains so much pain and hurt is nothing short of a miracle. So many people need to hear your story. Your words will change the world. I believe it with everything I am.

I love you so much.
Piper

To my readers, and all those affected by foster care and family separation, thank you for taking this journey with me. I hope you choose love in this life and are fueled with contagious hope. You're worthy of the space you claim, and your achievements are worth celebrating. I see you and the purpose brimming inside of you.

To those who have yet to feel chosen, wanting to be seen and begging to be heard, I see you. I hear you. You are more than what's happened to you. If no one has told you, your voice matters, and your stories and experiences are important.

There is a defiant flicker of resilience burning in your heart that refuses to be extinguished. With each setback, and each disappointment, dig deeper, and feel it all. Draw from the strength of your determination and belief that with God, healing is possible and within reach.

You, my friend, are an overcomer.

Made in United States
Orlando, FL
17 October 2024